HIDDEN RICHES

Edited by Eltin Griffin O CARM

Hidden Riches

THE EUCHARIST IN THE CARMELITE TRADITION

the columba press

First published in 2005 by
the columba press
55A Spruce Avenue, Stillorgan Industrial Park,
Blackrock, Co Dublin

Cover by Bill Bolger
The cover image is *Mary and the Carmelites* by Frances Biggs, a stained
glass window in the chapel of Terenure College, Dublin.
Origination by The Columba Press
Printed in Ireland by ColourBooks Ltd, Dublin

ISBN 1 85607 507 9

Table of Contents

Introduction

A very significant teaching of the Second Vatican Council is that the eucharist is the 'source and summit of the whole Christian life' (Church, *LG* 11). Of course this doctrinal statement has been true throughout the church's history right back to the Last Supper. However, the way in which the church has regarded the eucharist finds different expressions in each era and culture. The Carmelite Family has a rich eucharistic heritage that has been relatively hidden. It was, however, explored during the Year of the Eucharist in six lectures at the Gort Muire Spirituality Centre, Dublin in April-May 2005 which we are offering to a wider public.

Attendance at the eucharist was central for Carmelites from the beginning as the essay by Pat Mullins shows. The evolving later constitutional history of Carmelites shows an ever-increasing frequency about receiving holy communion. The early Constitutions of the Carmelite Order specified that all members of the community communicate seven or eight times a year; these were solemn occasions when all the brethren received the both host and chalice. Apart from these special community occasions they were also free to receive communion on Sundays and on the greater feasts. This legislation continued up to the Reformation, with communion generally becoming more frequent. Some communities of nuns received more frequently or less frequently than these norms. We see in Míceál O'Neill's paper that the Carmelite nun, St Mary Magdalene de' Pazzi (d. 1607) chose the convent at Florence, precisely because, unusually for the time, it had the custom of daily communion. Later the inroads of Jansenism would make communion less frequent.

Devotion to the eucharist is such a central feature of Roman Catholicism that people may not always be aware that it was only in the second millennium that it developed. In the first millennium one can say in a general way that the sacrament was reserved mostly for communion of the sick. Liturgy by the eleventh century had become more remote from the people, as Latin was no longer widely understood. People gradually sought devotional, rather than fuller liturgical participation. There was a great focus on the elevation and seeing the sacred host, which was seen as a form of spiritual communion. Priests were sometimes given stipends to prolong the elevation. There were other notable developments: prayer before the tabernacle is found in the thirteenth century; the feast of Corpus Christi was established in 1264 at the instigation of a remarkable nun, Bl Julienne de Mont-Cornillon (Juliana of Liège); processions of the blessed sacrament are found in Germany before 1311; benediction of the blessed sacrament as well as exposition apart from Mass arose from about the fourteenth century.

The sixteenth-century Reformers were especially critical of what they saw as a Catholic neglect of the words of the Lord 'take and eat'. Trent defended the legitimacy of eucharistic adoration, processions and the feast of Corpus Christi but insisted also on the reception of communion. Philip McParlan's contribution shows the eucharist as quite central in the formation that St Teresa of Avila gave to her reform.

The seventeenth and eighteenth centuries saw enormous development in exposition with huge monstrances, and the altar becoming more a royal throne than a table of offering. The devotion of forty hours continuous exposition had arisen in Italy in the sixteenth century. In these developments there were three main ideas. Adoration of the sacrament was seen as reparation for sacrileges committed against the eucharist. This was joined with an emphasis on devotion to the Sacred Heart and with remembrance of the Lord's reproach at Gethsemane, 'Could you not watch one hour with me?' (See Mark 14:37). Another thrust was exaltation of the eucharistic presence, adorers being as it were a guard of honour. With Charles de Foucauld we find the idea of the power of Christ's presence radiating from the consecrated bread. Eucharistic Congresses were well established by the turn of the century. They had originated with a meeting held in Lille through the exertions of Mgr Gaston de Ségur.

It is clear that from the seventeenth to the nineteenth centuries devotions were mostly focused on the presence of Christ rather than on the more profound theological reality, viz. the celebration, thanksgiving, anamnesis, memorial and paschal meal.

A final piece of background for the evolving Carmelite tradition is Jansenism, a movement centred in France and in the Low Countries, which stemmed from a book, *Augustinus*, published two years after the death of its author, Cornelius Otto Jansen (d. 1638). His disciples were extremely rigorist about salvation, about divine and church law and about sin. As a movement Jansenism had died out in the early years of the nineteenth century, but its spirit lingered, especially with regard to holy communion. There were two Jansenist teachings that did enormous damage. The first was that the prime reason for the existence of the blessed sacrament was to honour the majesty of God and give homage to God as the First Principle. The sanctification of the faithful was only a secondary reason for its institution. In Joseph Mothersill's article we see the strong reaction of St Thérèse of Lisieux against such views in her famous saying:

> It is not to remain in a golden ciborium that he comes down to us each day from heaven; it's to find another heaven, infinitely more dear to him than the first: the heaven of our soul, made to his image, the living temple of the adorable Trinity. (Ms A 48v)

The second harmful Jansenist teaching held that for the reception of holy communion perfect contrition was required. If the conditions for perfection contrition were then to be narrowly presented, many people would be afraid to risk receiving the sacrament. Such teaching gave rise to many scruples.

There was opposition to these Jansenist teachings particularly from Jesuits and from St Alphonsus Liguori (d. 1787). The latter favoured frequent Communion, and taught that the confessor should determine the number of times a particular person could receive it. This view was to be very influential. Another anti-Jansenist thrust in the church arose from the apparitions of the Sacred Heart to St Margaret Mary Alacoque (d. 1690). These apparitions favoured holy communion on the first Fridays, and the practice of the holy hour.

The emerging figure of Bl Elizabeth of the Trinity, outlined by Christopher O'Donnell, shows that this Carmelite drew together in a seamless whole the eucharistic practices of France and of her Order. Finally, we see the contemporary experience of the eucharist in the contemplative tradition of Carmel as exposed by Brian McKay and Sr Teresa Whelan.

Appearing in the Year of the Eucharist and coinciding with the Synod of Bishops' study of the eucharist, this book offers a wide readership a profound tradition of eucharistic spirituality, one that has not be treated extensively until now.

We present these papers beginning with the present-day contemplative experiences of the eucharist in Carmel. We then move backwards in time to examine the eucharistic life of some of the great figures of the Order: Thérèse of Lisieux, Elizabeth of the Trinity, Mary Magdalene of Pazzi and Teresa of Avila. We end with the place of the Mass in the foundation documents of the Carmelite Order, the way of life proposed to the hermits on Mount Carmel by St Albert of Jerusalem about 1210.

Eltin Griffin, O Carm,
Feast of Corpus Christi 2005

CHAPTER ONE

Eucharist and Contemplation

Brian McKay O Carm and Teresa Whelan ODC

a: Brian McKay O Carm

My presentation focuses on the re-discovery of the importance of contemplation for all the baptised, and how the eucharist can and does build up the life of contemplation in a practical way. I deal with the topic in four sections. In section one, I examine briefly the view of contemplation as presented by one spiritual writer. In section two, I explore the heart of contemplation from the perspective of the Carmelite Rule. In section three, I glance at contemporary attitudes to contemplation in Carmel. In section four, I attempt to show that the Roman Catholic understanding of eucharist does indeed nourish the insights into contemplation as presented.

Section One: Thomas Merton

The spiritual writer I have selected for the first section is actually outside the Carmelite tradition. I have three reasons for choosing Thomas Merton as my model. Firstly, he is writing within the living memory of most of us and so does not appear to be remote (as can be the case with authors from the distant past). Secondly, because he is writing about his own experience of contemplation, we can readily perceive that his awareness changes quite significantly with the passage of time. As we shall see, this development is of great interest to us. Thirdly, what contributed to this development of his understanding was his contact with Buddhism, and the inter-faith dimension of his thought is quite engaging.

As a young man, Thomas Merton (1915-1968) converted to Roman Catholicism and believed that he had a vocation to the contemplative life. Since this life was concerned with complete focusing on God and avoidance of that which might be superfluous (Merton's view), he sought a monastery of strict observance where he could give himself totally to the things of God and not be distracted. At the age of twenty-seven, he entered the Cistercian monastery in Kentucky where he found the environment to be most satisfactory for his needs. There were no newspapers, radios, and the silence was conducive to the journey inwards. His early years were very fruitful and that he was making significant progress was noticed by his abbot who called him in one day and suggested that Merton should write his autobiography as a help to other young people seeking the truth about life. Merton was horrified at the suggestion for, although he had trained as a writer, he had left such superfluous things at the monastery gate, and believed that such a venture would seriously interfere with his contemplative journey. He brought his concern to his spiritual director who reminded him that in the Cistercian tradition, obedience to the abbot was essential, and so the task was begun. His autobiography, *The Seven Story Mountain*, published in 1948, became a bestseller and Merton began to receive letters requesting his spiritual advice.

One year later, we find Merton publishing *Seeds of Contemplation* in which he presents his own experience of the journey inward. Here, Merton writes about finding who we are in God – a journey that requires self-emptying which leads to an abyss of freedom where we encounter Love. This encounter can only be achieved if we are prepared to leave behind the distractions of the world, and so seems to speak to a highly select group of people. Again, this publication was well received and more letters arrived at the monastery. Merton was in even greater turmoil since the reading of and answering these letters was itself a distraction from what he had entered the monastery to achieve.

More distractions were to follow. In 1951, he was made Master of Scholastics which entailed the training of those going forward for solemn vows and ordination. However, and of interest to us, in his new responsibility Merton discovered a 'new desert and the name of this desert is compassion'. This is an important point of transition in the life of Merton because he now sees that involvement with these people on their journey is part of his own journey of contemplation and not opposed to it as he formerly believed. Isolation from people is no longer the way to true contemplation. He begins to see that his work of writing and correspondence is intimately connected with contemplation and not at variance with the life of silence.

In the 1950s, Merton, almost by accident, came in contact with Eastern religions and Buddhism in particular, where the dichotomy between contemplation and action (*the* western problem of spirituality) quite simply does not exist. For the Buddhist, *all* experiences of daily life are subjects for meditation and all depends on one's attitude and ability to focus or centre. This insight was the missing link that Merton had been seeking, and so he could write, teach, lecture and still be deeply immersed in the life of contemplation. In 1962 he published *New Seeds of Contemplation* which, according to himself, was not merely a new edition but, in fact, a new book in which he acknowledged that contemplation is to be found within the context of ordinary life and appeals directly to experience. He introduces themes from the wisdom literature which emphasises the goodness of all creation and the values inherent in ordinary life. His new insight into the journey inward led him to write against nuclear war, the cold war and the Vietnam war since he believed that the contemplative is called to engagement with the world and to take prophetic stands when and where appropriate.

One can see from the above brief sketch that Merton's understanding of contemplation changed quite significantly from the 1940s to the 1960s. From avoidance of all that might corrupt or pollute the journey of contemplation, he came to believe that *every* experience can be (and should be) material for contemplation and thus, Merton demonstrates that all the baptised are called to be contemplatives as we journey along the daily road of life. Merton never denies the necessity of the enclosed religious way of life as a heightened living of contemplation, but he takes

pains to teach that contemplation is not the preserve of the few
but is open to all who wish to live life to the full. We do find in
Merton (and we must never ignore this vital point) that the person seeking the contemplative way *must* have a significant commitment to prayer and silence on a very regular basis. It is not
possible to undertake this journey inward without close intimacy
with the Lord and a great deal of listening, which requires inner
peace and silence. When Merton died in 1968, the world lost a
very busy and engaged contemplative.

Section Two: The Carmelite Rule
If I had asked my novice director to point me to the heart of contemplation in the Carmelite Rule when I was a novice, he would
have directed me to the chapter which states that 'each of you is
to stay in his own cell or nearby, pondering the Lord's law day
and night and keeping watch at his prayers unless attending to
some other duty.' This chapter is indeed concerned with contemplation but there is a problem. If this is *the* chapter on contemplation, then where do the other chapters fit in in relation to
this theme? The answer is far from clear and there has been a
great deal of exploration and study of the Rule in the last twenty
years to attempt to make the text more accessible. In 1999, the
Dutch Carmelite Kees Waaijman wrote *The Mystical Space of
Carmel* in which he attempts to explain how the chapters relate
to each other. He divides the Rule into four sections: the basic
provisions (having a prior, a place, a cell, a refectory), the elementary exercises (remaining in the cell, meditating on the word
of God, praying, keeping vigil, saying the psalms, coming together in the oratory and for chapter, listening in obedience), the
clothing with the spiritual armour, and the preservation of contemplation (work and silence). If he entitles the fourth section
the preservation of contemplation, then the implication is there
that all the preceeding sections are concerned with contemplation. In fact, for Waaijman, the heart of contemplation is to be
found in the chapter on the clothing with the spiritual armour.
Here I quote it in full: 'Since man's life on earth is a time of trial,

and all who would live devotedly in Christ must undergo persecution, and the devil your foe is on the prowl like a roaring lion looking for prey to devour, you must use every care to clothe yourselves in God's armour so that you may be ready to withstand the enemy's ambush. Your loins are to be girt with chastity, your breast fortified by holy meditations, for as scripture has it, holy meditation will save you. Put on holiness as your breastplate, and it will enable you to love the Lord your God with all your heart and soul and strength, and your neighbour as yourself. Faith must be your shield on all occasions, and with it you will be able to quench all the flaming missiles of the wicked one: there can be no pleasing God without faith; and the victory lies in this – your faith. On your head set the helmet of salvation, and so be sure of deliverance by our only Saviour, who sets his own free from their sins. The sword of the Spirit, the word of God must abound in your mouths and hearts. Let all you do have the Lord's word for accompaniment.'

There are several points worth making about this chapter. Firstly, there is in fact no trace of Pelagianism. (Pelagius believed that we could achieve salvation through our own effort. His views were deemed to be heretical.) It is God who clothes us with the spiritual armour, and this clothing is about the putting on of the attributes of God himself. This clothing leads to a transformation of the person which is gradual and ongoing, and is always God's gift. Secondly, this clothing cannot take place if the elementary exercises which in turn need the basic provisions are not being observed. To put it simply, the one who does not keep vigil, say the psalms etc. will never be able to receive the gift of clothing. Note the similar idea which we observed in Merton when he insisted on the necessity of prayer and silence for contemplation to take place. So in the Carmelite Rule, we can observe a progression from the very basic points of what we are given (a prior, a cell) to the reception of the gift of clothing which is at the heart of Carmelite spirituality. Thirdly and perhaps most importantly, we note that this clothing with the attributes of God centres around the theological virtues of charity, faith and hope (to use the order in which they appear in this chapter). In other words, the contemplative is the one who has put on charity, faith and hope and who therefore lives on a daily basis from the perspective that these virtues instil. Whether I am driving in rush hour traffic or whether I am doing the laundry or whatever I may be doing, it must be influenced by my clothing with charity, faith and hope. It strikes me as highly interesting that the virtue of hope is the one in third place. Perhaps it is the most important in our world today when many seem to live out of despair and a sense of absurdity. Is hope the gift of Carmel to all our sisters and brothers? It certainly is a powerful fruit of contemplation for it reminds us that *all* is in the hands of a loving God.

Whilst the Carmelite Rule was written for the hermits on Mount Carmel in the thirteenth century, it is clear that the dynamic of the Rule can be useful for all who wish to pursue the things of God. The key word which sums up what takes place as the clothing with the spiritual armour occurs on a daily basis is the word 'listening'. The one who learns to listen like Mary and Jesus himself through prayer and silence, and who is prepared to co-operate with the grace of God like St Thérèse of the Child Jesus, will *in God's time* be transformed into what God wants him / her to be. The very desire to embark upon such a journey of transformation is already what Carmel calls contemplation.

Section Three: Contemporary Carmel
In the years following the Second Vatican Council, religious orders went back to their roots in order to discover the best way of proceeding into the future. For Carmel, there was a re-discovery of what contemplation involved, for it had become down through the centuries the preserve of those who had the time and freedom to devote long hours to prayer. In 1983 at the conclusion of his twelve years as Prior General, Fr Falco Thuis published a book entitled *In Wonder at the Mystery of God* in which he presented a rather fresh approach to contemplation based upon what he had experienced during his time as General. Early in the

book he writes: 'every man ought to be a contemplative'. His point is that in the midst of a frenetic world which is regarded by many as an end in itself, all are called to become aware of what is transcendent within themselves and so become aware of what is transcendent in others. He states strongly that contemplation can never be about detachment from life or alienation from reality, but goes on to give a useful if somewhat novel definition of contemplation: 'It [contemplation] is a technical term for that vital reality which leads every man to the discovery of what it means to be himself.' (This is a direct quote so apologies for the sexist language.) In other words, it is only when I am living in right relationship with God and thus with others, that I can come to know who I am and what my place in the world should be. (One thinks of Thérèse's acceptance of her place as the Little Flower amidst all the other beautiful trees and plants. She realised that this was what God wanted and she didn't require anything more. One could say that she knew who she was.)

Thuis goes on to emphasise that continual attention to the word of God is vital for this awareness to grow. He points out that in *Gaudium et Spes,* no 36, it is clear that what God has created is both good and beautiful, and so in everyday reality humankind must be encouraged to see the hand of the creator at work. He states that deep within the being of every person, there is a strong sense of incompleteness which causes the individual to always want more out of life. This, he contends, is the longing that only union with God can satisfy, and the longing itself is the beginning of contemplation. This desire for more in the depth of the person's being is answered by the presence of the Holy Spirit who imparts the gift of wisdom. Most importantly from our perspective, he expresses the conviction that contemplation is open to all people. He writes: 'Contemplation is attained ... by every baptised person who has responded positively to the divine plan in his regard.' He also points out that this treasure is frequently to be found in very ordinary people who put it into practice in the little details of their daily lives.

So, as we reflect more and more on what contemplation is,

we realise that the call to be contemplatives is one addressed to all people. I keep emphasising this point for it is a point that is not always appreciated, and is a gift from God through Carmel for all the baptised.

Falco Thuis was writing in 1983. Now let us look briefly at the Carmelite Constitutions of 1995 to discern what is being said. Here, the essential charism is presented as being three-fold: prayer or contemplation, fraternity and service in the midst of the people. What is of interest to us is that contemplation appears to be an umbrella charism which includes and animates the other two. In article 17 of the Constitutions we read: 'Contemplation begins when we entrust ourselves to God, in whatever way he chooses to approach us: it is an attitude of openness to God whose presence we discover in all things.' This article continues by pointing out that contemplation is an experience of the love of God, an experience which 'empties us of our limited and imperfect human ways of thinking, loving and behaving, transforming them into divine ways'. Article 18 adds the following: 'The search for the face of God … makes us more attentive to the signs of the times and more sensitive to the seeds of the Word in history.'

In the 1995 Constitutions we find two ancient expressions that have been important for Carmelites down through the centuries and which continue to be operative in our own time: 'vacare Deo' and 'puritas cordis'. Vacare Deo translates literally as vacating for God. It is a significant part of the process of transformation for it disposes the individual to putting into practice what God wants in any situation. It entails being able to see reality with the eyes of God and so being enabled to act with integrity in any situation. Oftentimes, the reason why we cannot see as God sees is because our hearts have fallen in love with what is not wholesome. Puritas cordis or purity of heart is both a fruit and source of the process of transformation and allows us to discard whatever is not useful for the journey of life.

It is becoming clearer, then, that contemplation is about being immersed in reality in order to discover the presence of

God who is already in every person and situation. Hopefully you are agreeing with me in believing that this understanding of contemplation is both attractive and accessible to us all. We now must briefly explore the obstacles to the flourishing of this attractive interpretation. I summarise the obstacles into four groups. There may indeed be many more. I leave it to you to work it out for yourself.

My four are: prioritising, fear, idolatry and psychological baggage.

We are all busy people. Every day there are a thousand and one duties to be performed and time is precious. It can quite easily happen that amidst a very busy schedule, what goes to the wall is my prayer time. It must be clear from all that we have said thus far that if personal prayer goes to the wall, even for the best of reasons, the journey of transformation which is itself contemplation will suffer significantly. I cannot be a contemplative if I am not a person of regular intimacy with the Lord. In order to keep personal prayer alive in my life, I may need to re-establish my priorities. Not always either easy or pleasant, this insistence on a good prayer life is a non-negotiable.

Fear is a little less obvious. You may want to tell me that you are not afraid of anything. However, many of us are afraid of losing control of our lives. The contemplative comes to realise that God is in control and that there are times when we must be prepared to let go of our own ways of doing and looking. It is easy to talk about it but quite difficult to live. St Teresa of Avila wrote that many good people never make it beyond the third or fourth set of rooms in the Castle precisely because they are not prepared to surrender their wills and live in a consonance of desire with God. I worry because I am literally afraid of letting go. God may lead me to a place where I would rather not be. This obstacle is always about the issue of control.

Idolatry is even more complex. None of us wants to follow false gods, do we? Yet, in reality, we frequently take a good and ask it to be God. Fr John Welch, in his *Seasons of the Heart*, warns us that it is so easy to opt for a lesser god, and a lesser god means a lesser human being. He equates idolatry with addiction and notes that we are all addicted to something. He is most challenging when we writes: 'One can be addicted to obviously destructive things, but one can also be addicted to the church, addicted to the Pope, addicted to religious practices, even addicted to Carmel, and addicted to God as we create God to be.' We therefore can never afford to be complacent about this obstacle as it haunts us all the time. Only the grace of God can both identify and deal with the idols that we create around and within us.

Finally, I mention psychological baggage. What I mean by this is the shadow side of our personality that has a propensity to warp reality in such a way that we can not possibly see with the eyes of God. The carrying around of past hurts, wrongs and injuries that we have experienced on the journey can cause our vision to be altered in a destructive way and our belief in the goodness and beauty of God can literally be ruined. Again only the grace of God can alter our vision so that we can see as God sees.

I pass over the obstacles quickly for I sense that we all know of their existence and realise that only God can bring about the change that is needed. So, it is well time to ask where does our understanding of the eucharist fit in to what has been discussed thus far.

Section Four: The Eucharist
Since the chapter in the Rule on the eucharist is being treated of by Br Pat Mullins, I merely mention that in Kees Waaijman's schema of the Rule, the chapter on the eucharist is one of the elementary exercises. In other words, the daily eucharist is an essential part of the journey of transformation. I want to refer to two things: the 1992 *Catechism of the Catholic Church* and the liturgical prayers.

There is a most useful section in the catechism entitled *The Fruits of Holy Communion* in which we find much food for the journey of contemplation that we have described. In 1391 we read that 'the principal fruit of receiving the eucharist … is an intimate union with Christ Jesus'. In the eucharist, Christ literally christens us, that is, he changes us into what he wants us to be. This intimate union does at least two things for us: it helps us deal with our idolatry (we cannot be close to Christ without experiencing purification) and, in the love of Christ, all fear is driven out. Therefore, frequent reception of the eucharist removes (in God's time) two of the obstacles mentioned above.

1391 also refers to the fact that 'life and resurrection [are] conferred on whoever receives Christ'. The one who lives under the influence of the resurrection is the person of hope, and so we find that 1391 points towards the eucharist as the great assistance to being clothed with the theological virtue of hope.

1394 refers to the virtue of charity reminding us that 'the eucharist strengthens our charity … and this living charity wipes away venial sins'.

Our propensity towards sin is also dealt with by 1395 which notes that 'the more we share the life of Christ and progress in his friendship, the more difficult it is to break away from him by mortal sin'.

1397 further develops the upbuilding in charity since the eucharist 'commits us to the poor'.

1396, 1398, 1399 and 1400 all refer to the eucharist as *the* sacrament of unity, reminding us very powerfully that intimacy in Christ always leads to intimacy with others, even those of other denominations and faiths.

Finally, in 1381 we find reference to the virtue of faith. Not only is faith required to believe in the eucharist, but our faith is strengthened by our contact with the Lord. In short, we find that the teaching of our church as presented in the *Catechism* reinforces the idea that the journey requires that we be fed and the food that is needed is Jesus Christ himself really present in the eucharistic species (1374).

It is worth mentioning that in the Carmelite tradition, when we refer to the eucharist we are also thinking of the real presence of the Lord in his word. The Liturgy of the Eucharist and the Liturgy of the Word always go together.

What about liturgical texts? I wonder how often do we take notice of the prayer after communion? I suspect that most of us rarely if ever listen to this short prayer, and yet it points out very powerfully what we expect the eucharist to do for us. I cite five examples taken from the Eastertide liturgy.

Lord, may this Eucharist which we have celebrated in memory of your son, help us to grow in love. Note that, from our perspective, we are requesting that we be clothed with the theological virtue of charity. *Lord, may this celebration of our redemption help us in this life and lead us to eternal happiness.* When we pray for help in this life we are requesting that we be protected from negativity, idolatry and fear and that we be filled with what is positive. Again in this, I see reference to the theological virtues. *Merciful Father, may these mysteries give us new purpose and bring us to a new life in you.* The new purpose is the daily conversion that is required for us to follow the way of transformation. The reference to new life brings the virtue of hope to mind. *Almighty and ever-living Lord, you restored us to life by raising Christ from death. Strengthen us by this Easter sacrament; may we feel its saving power in our daily life.* Here we have reference to our need for food on a daily basis. The body cannot grow without nourishment; the journey of transformation needs the *panis angelorum. Lord, watch over those you have saved in Christ. May we who are redeemed by his suffering and death always rejoice in his resurrection for he is Lord for ever and ever.* The protection that the eucharist affords us and the joy and hope that it imparts is very evident in this final prayer.

To make my point again: when we read or hear these prayers with the eyes and ears of contemplatives, it is so obvious that the church is reminding us that we can never complete the journey without the bread of life, and that in the love that is freely given to us in this sacrament, the journey becomes a joy.

Four final points. Firstly, I want to remind you that in our tradition, the eucharist is always associated with medicine and so with healing. Every Mass is a healing Mass because it brings us into contact with the one who came not for those who were well but for those who needed the doctor. Our journey of transformation always requires healing so that we can continue refreshed.

Secondly, since the Mass is the representation of the sacrifice of Calvary, the grace that flows from this sacrament is more than we need for the ups and downs of our journey. When we attend with a listening heart to the sacred liturgy, the Lord does indeed lavish us with all the grace that we need to nourish our souls.

Thirdly, the contemplative is one who desires to rest in the Lord, and in eucharistic adoration we have the opportunity simply to be in his presence and to allow him to do with us what he wills.

Finally , we remind ourselves that the Mass is our anamnesis, that is, what we do so that we never forget what the Lord has done for us. In our celebration of the eucharist, we recall that we have been given every gift through the life, death and resurrection of Our Lord Jesus Christ and we eat his flesh and drink his blood until he comes in glory.

Since in the eucharist we have all that we need for our sustenance, we acknowledge that the journey of transformation needs Jesus who is the bread of life.

Bibliography:

Robert H. King, *Thomas Merton and Thich Nhat Hanh*, New York, London, Continuum, 2001

Falco J.Thuis, *In Wonder at the Mystery of God*, Rome, Carmelite Publications, 1983

Kees Waaijman, *The Mystical Space of Carmel*, Leuven, Peeters, 1999

John Welch, *Seasons of the Heart, The Spiritual Dynamic of the Carmelite Life*, Melbourne, Carmelite Communications, 2001

Catechism of the Catholic Church, Dublin, Veritas, 1994

Constitutions of the Order of the Brothers of the Blessed Virgin Mary Of Mount Carmel, Rome, Carmelite Publications, 1996

b: Teresa Whelan ODC

If I were to ask any of you to describe the air we breathe how easy would it be?

We are so used to it we don't even think about it. It's just the natural thing to do. I had that sort of experience when asked to put these few words together. As I began to think about it I realised that the Eucharist is at the very centre of my life both as a Carmelite and a Christian.

St Peter has this to say to the young Christian church – to the newly baptised:

You are a chosen race, a royal priesthood, a consecrated nation, a people set apart to sing the praises of God who called you out of the darkness into his wonderful light.

By our baptism we are all called to sing the praises of God, that is to prayer and eucharist. Prayer and eucharist in our daily lives become the spiritual air we breathe.

We are speaking here about prayer and eucharist in the Carmelite tradition. The Carmelite way of life is simply a more intense living of our baptismal consecration and so has a lot to say to all Christians. At baptism our parents asked for the gift of faith for us. Faith is nourished by prayer and the sacraments and especially by the eucharist, and it is in faith that we come to prayer and eucharist.

The Carmelite rule tells us that we should be keeping watch at our prayers, pondering the Lord's law day and night. The Carmelite saints have given us a wonderful image of who God is. Elijah, the prophet whom Carmelites look to as a model and from whom we take our motto – With zeal have I been zealous for the Lord God of Hosts – tells us in the 1st book of Kings: 'As the Lord God of Israel lives, in whose presence I stand.' St Teresa of Avila describes prayer as a conversation with one whom we know loves us, St Thérèse gives us the image of God as a loving father and Bl Elizabeth of the Trinity reminds us of the Blessed Trinity dwelling within us.

So it is into the presence of a great, all powerful, living and loving God that we come. I like to think of God as the 'Living God', and he did say 'I have come that you may have life and have it to the full.' It is into the presence of the living God we come. In fact prayer and eucharist are all about presence and life. The very fact that the Blessed Trinity is dwelling within us means that there is always prayer going on in our hearts. Contemplation brings us into an awareness of that prayer.

Now what are we Carmelites doing watching in prayer, pondering the Lord's law?

Time and again the scriptures exhort us to listen – Is 50:4-7: 'Each morning he wakes me to hear, to listen like a disciple. The Lord has opened my ear. Hear O Israel, listen for the voice of the Lord.' We read the scriptures and we listen. It is with the ear of our hearts that we listen. We allow God's word to sink into our hearts. We come into his presence in an attitude of reverence and docility in order to hear his word in our hearts. We come as we are, in thanksgiving, in praise, in sorrow or in pain.

Prayer makes us sensitive to the needs of others and docile to the Word of God.

In prayer we become submissive, we listen and hear the word. I am slow to use that word submissive but I mean it in the context of listening. Listening is a very active exercise, we are fully engaged by it, taking in what is being said and at the same time holding my reactions (as distinct from my response) at bay. At the annunciation Our Lady heard the message of the angel deep in her heart and responded with the words and attitude, 'Behold the handmaid of the Lord.' She agreed to all that God had planned for her life, whatever that might entail.

In prayer we come to know ourselves very well. Our faults and failings, our weaknesses, the dark deeds we ourselves are capable of, and it makes us ready to empathise and sympathise with our brothers and sisters who come to us for prayers. Listening in prayer tunes us to listen to those who come to us to pray for them. We make their prayers our own and bring them to the Lord.

I use the word prayer because the word contemplation scares

me off a bit. I feel that the word implies mystical experiences and such like. But for me contemplation is simply a very deep awareness of the presence of God. You have all had that experience. You know when you go up the mountains or there is a beautiful sunset and it all engulfs you and you just know that God is in this and he is fully alive and making all this happen.

Carmelite prayer tends to be individual by it's nature (the vocation of a Carmelite fosters a hermit side) but when we gather at the altar we join our prayer to that of the whole church and our brothers and sisters gathered with us.

The eucharist is the climax of our prayer. It is the great prayer of Jesus to his Father. His supreme sacrifice. When he tells us 'Do this in memory of me' he doesn't just mean consecrate the bread and wine, he means us to wash the feet of our brothers and sisters just as he has done. That is, we must love them as he has loved them. Then we can come and offer our gift at the altar. We gather all our prayers and needs into the eucharist. We come into the presence of the God who loves us, we confess our sins and ask pardon, we praise him and hear his word. We express all our needs and prayers, we offer our gifts, fruits of the earth and work of our hands. We enter into the great prayer of Jesus. We are united with him as he offers himself to the Father. Jesus to whom we have listened, to whom we have prayed, now becomes truly alive, flesh, blood, soul and divinity and gives himself to us. He invites us to communion with him. The Mass is ended, we are sent out to love and serve the Lord. We serve him by serving our brothers and sisters. Our lives centre on the eucharist, the living Jesus whom we carry with us throughout the day. The Eucharist becomes fruitful for us by the way we share it throughout the day.

The privilege and gift which prayer and eucharist are, demand that we share them with each other in a life of service.

To finish I would like to make my own a few sentences from our Holy Father Pope Benedict. 'Thus this path upon which my venerated predecessors went forward, I too intend to follow, concerned solely with proclaiming to the world the living presence of Christ. The eucharist (is) the heart of Christian life, and the source of the evangelising mission of the church ... The eucharist makes the Risen Christ constantly present, Christ who continues to give himself to us, calling us to participate in the banquet of his Body and Blood. From this full communion with him comes every other element of the life of the church, in the first place the communion among the faithful, the commitment to proclaim and give witness to the gospel, the ardour of charity towards all, especially towards the poor ...'

CHAPTER TWO

The Eucharist and St Thérèse of Lisieux

Joe Mothersill O Carm

Context

In order to appreciate the eucharistic spirituality of St Thérèse it is important to put a few things into context. Today, 17 May 2005 marks the 80th anniversary of the canonisation of St Thérèse of Lisieux by Pius XI. Had Thérèse been alive on that day, she would have been 52 years old. She was born on 2 January 1873 in Alençon in Normandy. She entered the Carmelite Convent of Lisieux at the young age of 15 and remained there until her death on 30 September 1897 at the age of 24. When we bear in mind her youthfulness and her lack of any formal theological training we cannot but be struck by the sheer depth of her spirituality.

Devotion to the blessed sacrament was very strong in the church into which Thérèse was born. The forty hours devotion, Corpus Christi processions, benediction, first Fridays and visits to the blessed sacrament were important parts of popular piety. However, the French church was still very much affected by Jansenism. Such emphasis was placed on the adoration of the blessed sacrament outside Mass that the primary purpose of the sacrament – that of uniting us with Christ – was sometimes in danger of being overlooked. A heavy emphasis on being worthy to receive communion led to many people being burdened with a lot of scruples and hence reluctance to receive frequently.[1] Rather than being a support or help for people in following Christ, holy communion was often seen as a reward for having followed Christ perfectly. The laws about fasting before holy communion were quite strict and this also discouraged frequent

---

1. O'Donnell, Christopher, O Carm. *Prayer: Insights from St Thérèse of Lisieux*, Dublin: Veritas 2001, pp 53-54

communion. So it was not usual for people to receive daily communion at this time. As we shall see, Thérèse's thought challenges the negative influences of Jansenism and anticipates many of the reforms that took place at the Second Vatican Council.

It is clear from her writings and from what others have written about her that the eucharist is central to the spirituality of St Thérèse. Yet, there is no one place in her writings where Thérèse has brought together all her thoughts about the eucharist as, for example, her beautiful poem *Why I love you, O! Mary* draws together her thoughts about the Blessed Virgin.[2] Rather we find references to the eucharist throughout her writings. In this paper, what I hope to do is to take some of the major themes in her spirituality and use them as a framework to draw together her rich understanding of the eucharist. I want to weave these themes together by considering her beautiful description of her first communion day because I understand this description as not only reflecting her memories of that very special day in her life but also expressing what receiving holy communion meant for her throughout her life. I also want to consider these themes within the broader context of the Carmelite tradition to which St Thérèse belongs. Finally, I want to draw some practical conclusions for our own time and our own understanding of the eucharist.

Desire

Our hearts are always hungry – we are prey to a myriad desires – as soon as we have satisfied one desire another starts clamouring for our attention – we are never satisfied. The Carmelite tradition sees these desires of ours as symptoms of a deeper desire – a hunger at the centre of the human heart that only God can satisfy – only God is enough. It advises us to withdraw into the desert – the desert is a situation where these clamouring de-

2. Kinney, Donald, OCD, 'Introduction to PN 25 – *My Desires Near Jesus Hidden in His Prison of Love*' in *The Poetry of St Thérèse of Lisieux*, trs Donald Kinney OCD, Centenary Edition, Washington DC: ICS Publications, 1996, p 132

sires simply cannot be satisfied – when we do this we find that this deeper desire surfaces in our hearts opening us up to God who alone can satisfy us.

Desire is, I believe, a key to understanding Thérèse's spirituality. *The Story of a Soul*, Thérèse's autobiography and spiritual testament, is shot through with longing – longing for God. In Manuscript B, the central portion of her autobiography, she writes very movingly of her desires to serve Christ as warrior, priest, apostle, doctor and martyr.[3] Yet a short time later, Thérèse writes to her sister, Marie of the Sacred Heart who had expressed her sadness that she did not feel these strong desires Thérèse had described: 'Dear Sister, how can you say after this that my desires are the sign of my love? ... Ah! I really feel that it is not this at all that pleases God in my little soul; what pleases him is that he sees me loving my littleness and my poverty, the blind hope that I have in his mercy ... That is my only treasure, dear Godmother, why would this treasure not be yours?' Further in this same letter Thérèse writes: 'The desire alone to be a victim suffices, but we must remain always poor and without strength, and this is the difficulty ...'[4] If I understand her correctly, what Thérèse is saying is that we cannot boast of our desires as if to say: 'I'm more holy than you because I desire God more' or 'I deserve God's love because of my strong desires.' We cannot earn God's love, we can only accept it as freely given. Our desires are not a sign of our love for God but an invitation from God to accept his love for us – a faint echo of God's great desire for each one of us. God draws us by these desires. It is by listening to them that we find strength and meaning in our lives. It is by allowing them to reveal our poverty – our lack of self-sufficiency – our littleness – that we open the door to God's love and allow it to flow through us – that we begin to learn the real meaning of love.

3. Thérèse of Lisieux, *The Story of a Soul: The Autobiography of Thérèse of Lisieux*, trs John Clarke, OCD. 2nd Ed. Washington DC: ICS Publications, 1976, p 192
4. *Thérèse of Lisieux, General Correspondence – Vol 2*, trs John Clarke OCD, Washington DC: ICS Publications, 1988, LT 197, p 999

It is clear from her own writings and from the memories of
those who knew her that Thérèse always had a deep desire to receive Jesus in holy communion. In her testimony before the
diocesan inquiry, her sister Marie recalled: 'Love of the eucharist
was one of the chief characteristics of her piety. In Carmel, her
main source of suffering was her inability to receive communion
daily. Some time before her death, she told Mother Marie de
Gonzague, who was afraid of daily communion: "Mother, when
I get to heaven, I will make you change your opinion." And that
is exactly what happened. After the Servant of God's death our
chaplain gave us communion every day, and Mother Marie de
Gonzague, far from been indignant as before, was very happy
about it.'[5] A short poem written by Thérèse in the final months
of her illness when it had become quite difficult for her to receive communion catches very beautifully the intensity of her
desire. It goes as follows:

You who know my extreme littleness,
You aren't afraid to lower yourself to me!
Come into my heart, O! white Host that I love,
Come into my heart, it longs for you!
Ah! I wish that your goodness
Would let me die of love after this favour.
Jesus! Hear the cry of my affection.
Come into my heart![6]

There is a strong sense of fulfilment in Thérèse 's description of
her first holy communion day. As I have said, I understand this
description to express not just her experience on this special day
but also what holy communion meant for her each time she received it – even if the experience was not so intense. When I read
her description, I get this sense of a small creature like a little
bird, worn out by all her struggles who has at last found peace
and rest. Thérèse writes: 'Ah! How sweet was that first kiss of

5. O'Mahony, Christopher, *St Thérèse of Lisieux by those who knew her*,
Dublin, Veritas, 1975, p 96
6. PS 8, 'You who know my Extreme Littleness' in *The Poetry of St
Thérèse of Lisieux*, p 233

Jesus! It was a kiss of love; I felt that I was loved, and I said: "I love you, and I give myself to you forever!" There were no demands made, no struggles, no sacrifices; for a long time now Jesus and poor little Thérèse looked at and understood each other. That day, it was no longer simply a look, it was a fusion; they were no longer two, Thérèse had vanished as a drop of water is lost in the immensity of the ocean. Jesus alone remained …'[7]

Shortly after 'the Christmas Grace' when Thérèse was just 14 years old she began to have a profound sense of Jesus' desire to love us, to give himself for us and to dwell with us. Her sister Céline testified as follows: 'One Sunday as she was closing her prayer book after Mass a picture of Jesus crucified stuck out in such a way that all she could see of it was one of Jesus' hands, pierced and bleeding. At that moment she had a strange inner feeling of seeing this blood drip to the ground and nobody bothering to collect it. She immediately resolved to remain at the foot of the cross, in order to collect the blood and turn it to good account for sinners.'[8] It was this experience that led Thérèse to pray for the conversion of the convicted murder Pranzini. In *The Story of a Soul*, Thérèse writes about this experience as follows: 'After this unique grace my desire to save souls grew each day, and I seemed to hear Jesus say to me what he said to the Samaritan woman: "Give me to drink!" It was a true interchange of love: to souls I was giving the blood of Jesus, to Jesus I was offering these same souls refreshed by the divine dew. I slaked his thirst and the more I gave him to drink, the more the thirst of my poor little soul increased, and it was this ardent thirst he was giving me as the most delightful drink of his love.'[9] At a time when many were still affected with Jansenism, which held that salvation was only for some and not for all, Thérèse was proclaiming that Jesus is athirst with love for us and his particular concern is for those who are lost or estranged from him.

Thérèse saw the eucharist as a profound expression of Jesus'

7. Thérèse of Lisieux, *The Story of a Soul*, p 77
8. O' Mahony, Christopher, *op. cit.*, p 130
9. Thérèse of Lisieux, *The Story of a Soul*, pp 100-101

love for us – his desire for us. In the eucharist Jesus gives himself in love for us and to us. In a letter to her cousin Marie Guerin, who was suffering from scruples and anxious about receiving communion, Thérèse, a young novice aged sixteen, writes: 'Oh, my darling, think, then, that Jesus is there in the tabernacle expressly for you, for you alone; he is burning with the desire to enter your heart...'[10]

Thérèse develops this thought in *The Story of a Soul* where she writes: 'It is not to remain in a golden ciborium that he comes to us each day from heaven; it's to find another heaven, infinitely more dear to him than the first: the heaven of our soul, made to his image, the living temple of the adorable Trinity!'[11] Thérèse expresses the same idea in many of her poems. For example, she writes in *My Desires near Jesus Hidden in His Prison of Love:*

To Jesus my soul is dearer
Than precious vessels of gold.[12]

And in *Jesus, My Beloved, Remember!* Thérèse writes:
O Bread of the exiled! Holy and Divine Host,
It is no longer I who live, but I live on your life.
Jesus, the golden ciborium
You prefer to all others
Is I![13]

The Eucharist then, is a meeting place of desires – God's great love for each of us that leads the Father to send his only Son who gives himself for us and to us, and our deep hunger for God that is both satisfied and yet deepened by this gift.

Transforming Union
In her poems, Thérèse does not use the word 'communion'; instead she uses words like 'to transform' or 'to change'.[14]

---

10. Thérèse of Lisieux, *General Correspondence – Vol 1*, trs John Clarke OCD, Washington DC: ICS Publications, 1982, LT 92 p 568
11. Thérèse of Lisieux, *The Story of a Soul*, p104
12. *The Poetry of Thérèse of Lisieux*, PN 25 p 134
13. Ibid, PN 24 p 130
14. Kinney, Donald OCD, 'Introduction to PN 25' in *op. cit.*, p 132

I find the words 'transforming union' a very powerful way of referring to the eucharist. The presence of Jesus in the eucharist is neither static nor passive – he is not 'just there'. His presence is dynamic and active – he is present as giving himself – as reaching out in love. We find this truth expressed in Thérèse's poem *Heaven for Me* where she writes:

Oh! What a happy moment when in your tenderness
You come, my Beloved, to transform me into yourself.
That union of love, that ineffable intoxication,
That is Heaven for me![15]

In her poem *The Sacristans of Carmel,* Thérèse writes:

We are also hosts
Which Jesus wants to change into himself.[16]

In her description of her first communion day we also find her writing of a transforming union – a fusion. I think we have to approach this language with great care – Thérèse is seeking to express in words a very deep spiritual reality. In no sense does this union imply the destruction of the individual as if we just become absorbed into God and lose our identity. Rather this union implies our complete fulfilment – that we truly become ourselves and realise our identity fully. Perhaps we can understand this truth more clearly by considering what Thérèse called her 'Christmas Grace'.

After the death of her mother in 1877 Thérèse had become very sensitive and the slightest upset caused her great anguish so that she was often in tears. On Christmas night 1886 just a few days before her 14th birthday, Thérèse went with her father and Céline to midnight Mass. On their return Thérèse was on her way upstairs to take off her coat when her father made a comment about her still expecting to get presents left in her shoe on Christmas night – like children today getting their stockings filled by Santa. To the surprise of everyone including Thérèse herself – she did not take offence at his remarks but continued to

---

15. *The Poetry of Thérèse of Lisieux*, PN 32. p 153
16. Ibid, PN 40 p 171

be happy and cheerful. This incident marked a complete change in her life – she found a new freedom and was no longer over-whelmed by her feelings. She expresses it in these words: 'God was able in a very short time to extricate me from the very nar-row circle in which I was turning without knowing how to come out.'[17] Although in the brief way in which I have described it, this incident might seem trivial, anyone who has suffered in a similar way will realise just what a tremendous healing this in-volved for Thérèse – all at once she found her own strength and her own freedom. Thérèse understood that this healing came from the eucharist – she writes: 'We had come back from Midnight Mass where I had the happiness of receiving the strong and powerful God.'[18]

In her description of her first communion day, Thérèse writes that having received communion she began to cry. Those around her misunderstood what was happening and thought that she was sad because her mother had died and was not with her. Thérèse explains that rather than being overcome with sad-ness she was overcome with joy. She writes: 'They did not un-derstand that all the joy of heaven having entered my heart, this exiled heart was unable to bear it without shedding tears. Oh no the absence of Mamma didn't cause me any sorrow on the day of my first communion. Wasn't heaven itself in my soul, and hadn't Mamma taken her place there a long time ago.'[19] This must have been a moment of great healing for Thérèse who had suffered so much because of the death of her mother at a young age.

After her first communion, Thérèse received as frequently as her confessor permitted her. She describes how there grew within her a great desire to suffer for Jesus. She writes: 'Up until this time, I had suffered without loving suffering, but since this day I felt a real love for it. I also felt the desire of loving only God, of

17. Thérèse of Lisieux, *The Story of a Soul*, p 101
18. Ibid, p 99
19. Ibid, pp 77-78

finding my joy only in him.'[20] Without going too much into
Thérèse's attitude to suffering, I think we can see here another
example of deep healing in her life through the eucharist. She is
no longer paralysed by the fear of suffering as so many of us are
but she is freed to embrace life in its fullness which of necessity
includes suffering.

Thérèse clearly shows us the healing power of the eucharist
and she teaches us that this healing power springs from the
transforming union that this sacrament achieves. The eucharist
is healing because in it the deepest hungers of the human heart
are satisfied and we find our true meaning and purpose.

Sacrifice
In the Old Testament, a sacrifice was a ritual that expressed the
people's dedication to God. The sacrifice of the cross was not a
ritual sacrifice celebrated in the Temple but it is the perfect sacrifice because it expresses totally all that the Old Testament sacrifices sought to express. The Mass is not another sacrifice in addition to the sacrifice of Calvary. We speak of the sacrifice of the
Mass because the Mass makes present the sacrifice of the cross.
When we receive holy communion we are united with this sacrifice. If we separate sacrifice and communion we numb ourselves
to the power of the sacrament – the power of Jesus' self-giving
love – and there is the danger that Mass becomes for us either a
ritual we perform – something *we* do or a kind of fellowship
meal where we look back at Jesus as a figure in the past and remember him.

There is a very beautiful passage in Raymond Moloney's
book *Our Splendid Eucharist* in which he deals with the concepts
of communion and sacrifice; he writes as follows:

Christ giving himself is really what Calvary was. On the
cross Christ gave himself to the Father and he gave himself to
us: it was in giving himself to the Father that he gave himself
to us; and it was in giving himself to us that he gave himself
to the Father – two aspects of the one action. We might sum it

20. Ibid, p 79

up by saying that in the sacrifice Christ shows that he is giving himself to the Father and in holy communion he shows that he is giving himself to us. This giving of himself is the action in which Calvary becomes present in the Mass.[21]

In a very profound way, Thérèse lived out this connection between communion and sacrifice. At the core of her spirituality is an understanding of the incredible, infinite love of God for each one of us. God is forever reaching out to us with love, drawing us to him. We have only to open our hearts, to say 'yes' to his love. We have, as it were, to get out of the way and let God love us. For Thérèse, saying 'yes' to God's love involves making an effort to love in our turn. As she writes 'love is proved by works.'[22] Understood in this way, our small acts of love are not efforts to win God's love, we do not have to earn that love – it is given freely – rather they are a response to that love and so we do not have to be disappointed at their smallness or at our many failures because so long as we keep turning back to God's love, our small efforts take on infinite value and meaning. Letting God love us means letting God's love flow through us and transform us – so that it is not I who love but God who loves through me, (cf Gal 2:20). In *The Story of a Soul*, Thérèse writes: 'Yes, My Beloved, this is how my life will be consumed. I have no other means of proving my love for you other than that of strewing flowers, that is, not allowing one little sacrifice to escape, not one look, one word, profiting by all the smallest things and doing them through love.'[23] We know how radically Thérèse lived this out – taking every opportunity to show love. This insight of Thérèse brings us to the very heart of the mystery of the cross. The meaning of the cross lies not so much in the sufferings Jesus endured as in the love with which he endured them. Thérèse shows us how we are called to live out the sacrifice of the Mass – the sacrifice of Calvary, in our daily lives. This is beautifully ex-

---

21. Moloney, Raymond SJ, *Our Splendid Eucharist*, Dublin, Veritas 2003, p 85
22. Thérèse of Lisieux, *The Story of a Soul*, p 196
23. Ibid

pressed in her poem *My Desires near Jesus hidden in His Prison of Love:*

> Jesus, Holy and Sacred Vine,
> O my Divine King, You know
> I am a cluster of golden grapes
> Which must disappear for you.
> Under the wine press of suffering,
> I shall prove my love for you.
> I want no other joy
> Than to sacrifice myself each day.
>
> Ah! What joy, I am chosen
> Among the grains of pure Wheat
> Who lose their lives for Jesus ...
> My delight is truly great! ...
> I am your dear spouse,
> My Beloved, come live in me,
> Oh! Come, your beauty has ravished me.
> Deign to transform me into You! ...[24]

In the popular piety of the time there was the practice of offering oneself as a victim to divine justice. The idea was to accept on oneself the punishments deserved by sinners. Thérèse was never attracted to this practice; instead she felt called to offer herself to merciful love – to accept fully the love of Jesus that is so often rejected by us. As O'Donnell writes: 'Here Thérèse touches almost accidentally on a most profound truth that is rarely noted with such clarity elsewhere in the history of spirituality: the most intense love for God consists in letting him fully love us.'[25] In her *Act of Oblation to Merciful Love*, Thérèse writes: 'In order to live in one perfect single act of Love, I OFFER MYSELF AS A VICTIM OF HOLOCAUST TO YOUR MERCIFUL LOVE, asking you to consume me incessantly, allowing the waves of infinite tenderness shut up within you to overflow into

---

24. *The Poetry of Saint Thérèse of Lisieux*, PN 25 pp 134-135
25. O'Donnell, Christopher O Carm, *Love in the Heart of the Church: The Mission of Thérèse of Lisieux*, Dublin, Veritas, 1997, p 38

my soul, and that thus I may become a martyr for your Love, O my God!'[26] The prayer as a whole has a Trinitarian structure. Thérèse is asking to be caught up in the love of the Trinity – in effect she is asking that she might love with Christ's love. A little earlier in the same prayer she says: 'I feel in my heart immense desires and it is with confidence I ask you to come and take possession of my soul. Ah! I cannot receive holy communion as often as I desire, but, Lord, are you not all-powerful? Remain in me as in a tabernacle and never separate yourself from your little victim.'[27]

What I find extraordinary about this prayer is the way Thérèse can take a word or idea in common use and by shifting our focus enable us to understand it in a renewed and purified way. This explains why we have to be so careful reading Thérèse because we can so easily misunderstand what she means by words like 'victim' or 'offering'. Clearly a victim of divine love is something different from a victim of crime!

When we receive holy communion we are being drawn into the love of the Trinity – into the self-giving love of Jesus. We are being invited to let ourselves be loved and to allow that love to flow through us to others. The words of Thérèse writing about her vocation seem very appropriate here: 'Yes, in order that love be fully satisfied, it is necessary that it lower itself, and that it lower itself to nothingness and transform this nothingness into fire.'[28]

Love
In *The Story of a Soul*, Thérèse reflects on the new commandment Jesus gives his disciples: to love one another as he has loved us, (cf Jn 15:12). She writes: 'Ah! Lord, I know you don't command the impossible. You know better than I do my weakness and imperfection; you know very well that never would I be able to love my sisters as you love them, unless you, O my Jesus, loved

26. Thérèse of Lisieux, *The Story of a Soul*, p 277
27. Ibid, p 275
28. Ibid, p 195

them in me. It is because you wanted to give me this grace that you made your new commandment. Oh! How I love this new commandment since it gives me the assurance that your will is to love in me all those you command me to love.'[29]

In her poem *Living on Love*, composed by Thérèse while at prayer before the blessed sacrament, she writes:

Living on Love is living on your life,
Glorious King, delight of the elect.
You live for me, hidden in a host.
I want to hide myself for you, O Jesus!'[30]

Thérèse goes on to pray that every aspect of her life, living in community, interceding for sinners and for priests, her suffering, illness and especially her death, might be lived out in love. In her last illness, when she received holy communion on 16 July – Sr Marie of the Eucharist sang stanza 14 of this poem – as a prayer after communion. It goes:

Dying of love is a truly sweet martyrdom,
And that is the one I wish to suffer.
O Cherubim! Tune your lyre,
For I sense my exile is about to end! ...
Flame of Love, consume me unceasingly.
Life of an instant, your burden is so heavy to me!
Divine Jesus, make my dream come true:
To die of Love! ...[31]

Thérèse did not receive communion passively, rather receiving communion impelled her to reach out to others with love. Her sister, Sr Agnes, records the following incident that occurred during Thérèse 's illness: 'It was afternoon. She had hardly any time to make her thanksgiving when some sisters came to see her. She told me in the evening: "How they came to disturb me after communion! They stared me in the face ... but in order not to be provoked, I thought of Our Lord, who retreated into soli-

29. Ibid, pp 220-221
30. *The Poetry of Saint Thérèse of Lisieux*, PN 17 p 90
31. Ibid, PN 17 p 92

tude and was unable to prevent the people from following him there. And he didn't send them away. I wanted to imitate him by receiving the sisters kindly".'[32]

One of the aspects of Thérèse's spirituality I find most attractive is the way she uses very simple everyday examples like the one above to teach us what she means. One of the purposes of the sacrament of holy communion is that we become another Christ – and that is exactly the mystery that Thérèse sought to live out.

Food for the Journey

Despite her great love of the eucharist Thérèse reports that she seldom received consolations when praying after receiving communion – in fact she writes that this was a period when she received least. True to the teachings of John of the Cross and Teresa of Avila, this lack of consolation did not worry Thérèse, as in her prayer she sought to please God rather than looking for consolations for herself.[33] In *The Story of a Soul*, Thérèse tells us how she prepared to receive holy communion: 'When I am preparing for holy communion, I picture my soul as a [free] piece of land and I beg the Blessed Virgin to remove from it any rubbish that would prevent it from being free; then I ask her to set up a huge tent worthy of heaven, adorning it with her own jewellery; finally, I invite all the angels and saints to come and conduct a magnificent concert there. It seems to me that when Jesus descends into my heart he is content to find himself so well received and I, too, am content. All this, however, does not prevent both distractions and sleepiness from visiting me, but at the end of the thanksgiving when I see that I've made it so badly I make a resolution to be thankful all through the rest of the day.'[34]

This is a very rich passage. We find here a familiar Carmelite

32. *St Thérèse of Lisieux – her last conversations*, trs John Clarke OCD, Washington DC, ICS Publications, 1977, p 121
33. O'Donnell, Christopher O Carm, *Prayer: Insights from St Thérèse of Lisieux*, pp 60-61
34. Thérèse of Lisieux, *The Story of a Soul*, pp 172 – 173. Cf O'Donnell Christopher O Carm, *Prayer: Insights from St Thérèse of Lisieux*, p 61.

theme of having one's heart empty for God – empty so that God can fill it – sometimes called in the Carmelite tradition: 'vacare Deo'. We also find a very strong sense of the communion of saints and indeed angels! There is nothing private about Thérèse's faith – she goes to God as a member of a community – a family – the church. This is also brought out in the way Thérèse prayed for the conversion of sinners, for example Pranzini. There is an understanding of the person becoming a tabernacle – a tent of God's presence in the world. It is worth noticing that all our Eucharistic Prayers have a strong emphasis on the communion of saints. Notice also how for Thérèse, holy communion is already a foretaste of heaven – the entire heavenly court is in her heart. Thérèse understands our reception of holy communion as anticipating sacramentally our future glory and as preparing us for that glory. The same understanding is found in Thérèse's poem *The Divine Dew*. This poem is a profound meditation on the mystery of the incarnation. It takes as its starting point an image used by St Augustine that Thérèse would have known from Dom Gueranger's *The Liturgical Year*. Since a small baby cannot digest ordinary food the mother transforms the food she eats into her own milk thus providing the child with sweet nourishment that can be digested. This is the image Augustine uses for the mystery of the incarnation – the Word of God coming to us in a form we can understand. The last stanza of Thérèse's poem reads:

> The seraphim feeds on glory.
> In Paradise his joy is full.
> Weak child that I am, I only see in the ciborium
> The colour and figure of Milk.
> But that is the Milk a child needs,
> And Jesus' Love is beyond compare.
> O tender Love! Unfathomable power,
> My white Host is Virginal Milk.[35]

The eucharist is food for our journey to God giving us the strength we need to grow in his likeness. The word eucharist

35. *The Poetry of Saint Thérèse of Lisieux*, PN 1 p 38

means 'thanksgiving' – accepting gladly a gift that is freely given. Thérèse's whole spirituality is eucharistic – accepting with open hands and childlike confidence the love of the all-powerful God.

Conclusion

Karl Rahner has said that 'the mystics differ from us in degree but not in kind.' The experiences that they undergo are human experiences, they do not belong to a different species or to some select sub-group separated from the rest of humanity. They are gifts to us – signs of what we are called to be. The mystics teach us that union with God is the ultimate goal of the spiritual journey. In her description of her first holy communion, Thérèse speaks of 'a fusion'. This is very strong language and Thérèse, familiar with the writings of Teresa and John, would have known this. I believe that Thérèse is telling us that this deep union is not the exclusive reserve of a few great saints but rather that we are all called to this union through our baptism and that in the eucharist we sacramentally anticipate at some level this deep union. Union with God is not a prize we have to win – indeed none of us could hope ever to do so – rather it is a free gift we can only accept with joy and gratitude. Carmelite spirituality emphasises again and again that we are all called to holiness – to union with God.

To summarise, Thérèse teaches us:
- To come to the eucharist hungry for God
- To want the eucharist to transform us into Christ
- To live out the eucharist by acts of self-giving love
- To want Jesus to love others through us
- To recognise ourselves in the communion of saints
- To recognise that heaven is already in our hearts
- To have a eucharistic attitude – joyfully accepting God's freely given love.

CHAPTER THREE

The Eucharist and Elizabeth of the Trinity (1880-1906)

Christopher O'Donnell O Carm

The eucharist is a vital and central Carmelite value. One can be surprised that Carmelite writers do not treat the sacrament frequently; it is always, however, presumed. It is the quality of the treatment rather than the quantity that is important. In Elizabeth of the Trinity there is a profound eucharistic doctrine. She is not that well known in the English-speaking world. However, with her centenary approaching, we can expect much more interest in this remarkable nun.

We begin with a few key dates and biographical details. Elizabeth Catez, who took the religious name of Elizabeth of the Trinity, sometimes also called Elizabeth of Dijon, was born 18 July 1880 at the military camp of Avor where her father Joseph Catez was stationed in the region of Cher. She was the first child of Marie Rolland. Later there would be another daughter, Marguerite. Her mother would not hear of her entering Carmel in her teens, so it would be 1901 before she went to the Dijon Carmel at the age of twenty-one. She died on the 9 November 1906 at the age of twenty-six, suffering from the then incurable Addison's disease.[1] She left as writings four spiritual treatises, 346 letters, journals and retreat notes and 123 poems.[2] Many

1. *The Complete Works of Elizabeth of the Trinity*, Vol 2, Washington, ICS, 1995, 256.
2. The works of Elizabeth are in one French volume: *Oeuvres complètes: Édition critique par Conrad de Meester*, Paris, Cerf, 1991, abbreviated OeuvC. English trs, *The Complete Works of Elizabeth of the Trinity*, 3 vols, Washington, ICS, 1984, 1995, vol 3 still awaited)—abbrev. Works followed by volume number, page. The following abbreviations are now standard for the works of Elizabeth: CF *Le ciel dans la foi* ('Heaven in Faith' = Spiritual Treatise 1); DR *Dernier retraite* ('Last Retreat,' =

people will know of her great prayer, 'O my God, Trinity whom I adore.'

Conversion

Many of the saints had serious character flaws from which they were delivered by God's grace. They all experienced a profound conversion, and had afterwards to keep struggling to maintain the healing to which God had brought them.

Elizabeth of Dijon was an extremely gifted musician, and might have made a career as performer or teacher of the piano. Like Thérèse in childhood she showed some signs of precocious piety. But she was subject to outbursts of violent rage. From the time of her first confession at the age of seven she tried to take herself seriously in hand. In fact she would later speak of this as her 'conversion'. When she was thirteen, like Thérèse and at about the same age, she too had a serious bout of scruples. Indeed we can see the years from her first confession to about the age of eighteen as a time of grave spiritual struggle. We can see in the part of her diary, which has come down to us, covering only two years before she entered Carmel (1899-1900) that from that time there is a significant spiritual growth. She also notes that she was reading St Teresa of Avila's *Way of Perfection*.[3]

She was then deeply touched by the grace of God, to which she responded with generosity. She did not, however, escape the law of the spiritual life that growth in holiness is gradual, painful and always precarious. She was marked by that great determination and strength of will without which there is no genuine holiness.

Spiritual Treatise 3), GV *La grandeur de notre vocation* ('The Greatness of Our Vocation' = Spiritual Treatise 2); J *Journal* (Diary); L *Lettres* (Letters identified by number); LA *Laisse-toi aimer* ('Let Yourself Be Loved' = Spiritual Treatise 4); NI *Notes intimes* (Personal Notes); P *Poèsies* (Poems); S *Souvenirs* (documents on Elizabeth published in 1909 by the Carmel of Dijon).
3. *Journal* 20 February 1899 – OeuvC 816-817; see Spiritual Doctrine 9

Studies on Elizabeth

Elizabeth has been in the shade of Thérèse of Lisieux, whom she admired greatly and whose *Story of a Soul* she had read in 1899. There has not been much serious study about her, though dissertations are beginning to appear. However, with the centenary in 2006 one can expect more interest, especially a major study promised from Fr Conrad De Meester, who has edited her works in a critical edition.

The first significant presentation of Elizabeth's life and doctrine was by the Dominican Fr M. M. Philipon, *The Spiritual Doctrine of Elizabeth of the Trinity*, first published in English in 1947.[4] In the early 1950s Hans Urs von Balthasar wrote two ground-breaking studies on Thérèse and Elizabeth, which he later combined in a book called, *Two Sisters in the Spirit: Thérèse of Lisieux and Elizabeth of the Trinity*.[5] The first edition of the Thérèse book was in 1950, then entitled: (*Thérèse von Lisieux: Geschichte einer Sendung* soon translated into English as *St Thérèse of Lisieux: Story of a Mission* (1954). The volume on Elizabeth appeared in German as *Elizabeth von Dijon und ihre geistliche Sendung* (*Elizabeth of Dijon and her Spiritual Mission*).[6] A substantial literature of popular books and articles is now building up especially in French and Italian.[7] There is little on Elizabeth and the eucharist.

Her significance

Since the study of Balthasar, there is a growing interest in Elizabeth, and some awareness that she is a major spiritual writer. Unlike Thérèse, with whom comparisons are inevitable, Elizabeth has left significant writings before her entry to Carmel

---

4. Frequently reprinted, e.g. Washington, DC, Teresian Charism Press, 1987

5. San Francisco, Ignatius, 1992, from *Schwestern im Geist*, Einsiedeln, Johannes Verlag, 1970

6. Cologne and Olten, Hegner, 1952; English *Elizabeth of Dijon: An Interpretation of her Spiritual Mission*, New York, Pantheon, 1956

7. A major one is A. Sicari, *Elisabetta della Trinità: Un esistenza teologica*, Rome, Ed. OCD, 1986

in 1901: her early letters (1-88), her poems which date from her fourteenth year (1-72) as well as her diary kept over two years 1899-1900. Elizabeth's prioress, Mother Germaine was in no doubt concerning the influence of Thérèse: 'The Mistress of Novices at Lisieux was also that of the Dijon Carmel, where her portrait presides.'[8]

We cannot deal here with her relationship to Thérèse, the similarity and the dissimilarity between them.[9] One can say at least that her explorations into Trinitarian life and perhaps also her doctrine of suffering as well as her grasp of the contemplative dimension of Carmel may be more profound than her sister of Lisieux. We will see too that Elizabeth's eucharistic doctrine ranges beyond Thérèse's. Any study of Elizabeth has to take into account the vocation that she gradually appropriated as to be 'The Praise of Glory,' (see Eph 1:12, 14 – *Laus Gloriae* which she erroneously cited as *Laudem*). We find it first in letters from 1904, in November 1905, and she used it occasionally as a personal name.[10] The second indispensable theme is her teaching on the Trinity and on the divine indwelling.[11] These, we will see, encase her eucharistic teaching.

Her Carmelite vision

To a close friend, Germaine de Gemeaux, who had thoughts of becoming a Carmelite, Elizabeth wrote:

A Carmelite, my darling, is a soul who has gazed on the Crucified, who has seen him offering himself to his Father as a victim for souls and, recollecting herself in this great vision of the charity of Christ, has understood the passionate love of his soul, and has wanted to give herself as he did ... And on the mountain of Carmel, in silence, in solitude, in prayer that never ends, for it continues throughout everything, the

8. Cited by De Meester, Works 2:86
9. See De Meester, Works 1:25-38 for some insights. Her first reference to Thérèse is L. 172/Works 2:115-118 (to Germaine de Gemeaux, 20.8.1903)
10. See L 260/Works 2:245 (4 January 1906)
11. See De Meester Works 1:25-26; Sicari, *Elizabetta* 147-163

Carmelite lives as if in heaven: '*by God alone.*' The same One
who will one day be her beatitude and will fully satisfy her in
glory is already giving himself to her. He never leaves her, he
dwells within her soul; more than that, the two of them are
one. So she hungers for silence that she may always listen,
penetrate more deeply into his Infinite Being. She identifies
with him whom she loves, she finds him everywhere; she
sees him shining through all things! Is not this heaven on
earth? You carry this heaven within your soul.[12]

We could remark in passing on the words she underlines and
places in inverted commas, *Dieu seul (God alone).* The phrase has
an important history in French spirituality; it goes back to Henri
Boudon (d. 1702) whose works were very popular in France and
very influential in Saint-Sulpice; this Parisian seminary had an
immense direct and indirect role in the training of the French
clergy. One could suspect that Elizabeth would often have heard
the phrase in sermons, but there may be a stronger influence
from an earlier century. The reality of Boudon's disinterested
love of God alone is certainly at the heart of Elizabeth's spirituality, whatever about the actual phrase. We cannot, of course, forget the memorable saying of St Teresa of Avila, *Solo Dios basta
(God alone is enough)*, which would surely have been known to
Elizabeth. The influence of the French School of spirituality will
emerge later as we study Elizabeth's eucharistic spirituality.

To her mother she wrote two months before her profession
(January 1903):

The Lamb whom the blessed adore in the [beatific] Vision is
the One to whom your Elizabeth is betrothed and the One
whose bride she so longs to become. Oh! Mama, how beautiful my part is. The whole divine world is mine, for it is the

12. L 133/Works 2:61-62 (7.8.1902); see also L 136/Works 2:65-66
(14.9.1902); also L 149 shortly before her profession Works 2:81-2; NI
14/OeuvC 906-907; she also wrote a number of poems about Carmel
even before she entered, P 38/OeuvC 946-947; P 40-41/OeuvC 950-952;
P 45/OeuvC 956-957P 86/OeuvC 1009-1010. See Sicari, *Elizabetta* 111-
134.

centre in which I must live and, already here below, I must follow the Lamb everywhere.[13]

In a letter she cites the Carmelite motto and comments:

If you wish, our souls passing through space, will meet to sing in unison that great motto of our Father [Elijah]; we will ask him on his feast day for the gift of prayer that is the essence of the life in Carmel, that heart-to-heart that never ends, because, when we love, we belong no longer to ourselves but to the one we love, and we live more in Him than in ourselves.[14]

She also gave some memorable brief summaries of the essence of Carmel: 'I could answer that, for the Carmelite there is only one occupation: "to love, to pray".'[15] Again, 'The essence of our life in Carmel is this divine, wholly intimate union; it is what makes our solitude so precious.'[16] Still more succinctly, 'I think that the Carmelite actually draws her happiness from this divine source: faith.'[17] Like Thérèse she felt her heart expand in Carmel.[18] Some background will be helpful in exploring Elizabeth's eucharistic doctrine.

Eucharist at the time of Elizabeth

A double background, Carmelite and French, needs to be kept in mind as we consider Bl Elizabeth's practice and thoughts about the eucharist. The practice of frequency varied a good deal in French Carmels. We know that daily communion was not customary in the Lisieux Carmel. Permission for reception rested with the confessor and to an extent with the Carmelite superior. In 1890 the Vatican Congregation of Bishops and Religious had decreed that if the confessor allowed frequent, even daily com-

13. L 143/Works 2:74 (1.11.1902)
14. L 229/Works 2:308 (to an unknown male Carmelite novice who did not persevere, 17.7.1906)
15. L 168/Works 2:108 (to M de Angles, 1.11.1902)
16. L 184/Works 2:134 (to M de Angles, 24.11.190)
17. L 236/Works 2:210 (to her mother 11/12.8. 1905)
18. 'If only you knew how one's heart expands in Carmel.' L 180/ Works 2:129 (to M de Lignin, 23.9.1903)

munion, the religious superior was not to interfere. Soon it
would no longer be an issue in the church: in 1905 Pope St Pius X
issued a decree 'On Frequent Communion.'[19] The year before
was a very important one for Elizabeth's growth. It saw the encyclical of St Pius X, 'To restore all things in Christ.' In that year
too we find the first reference to Elizabeth's central spiritual in-
tuition, 'the Praise of Glory' (Eph 1:12),[20] and the great prayer
'Trinity whom I adore.'[21] Daily communion only became possible with the decree of Pope St Pius X (20 December 1905). Even
then the priest could not enter the cloister to give communion;
Elizabeth was carried by the sturdy Sister Marie of the Holy
Spirit to the grille in her final illness.[22]

First Communion
Like Thérèse of Lisieux Elizabeth longed for the day of her first
communion. In a child's letter she asks God to make her good as
she was approaching it.[23] She said on that day: 'I am no longer
hungry, Jesus has fed me.' The Prioress of Carmel told her on
that day the meaning of her name, 'House of God'.

A key to this day is her poem, *The Anniversary of my First
Communion*[24] written some months before she entered Carmel. It
begins in classical terms asking birds, sea, sky, and all the works
of God to unite in praising God. In this rather literal translation
italics have been used to indicate themes that will be significant
and developed in her more mature writings.

A thankful and *joyous* hymn
A hymn which will sing of my love
On the anniversary of that day.
When Jesus *took up his dwelling in me*,
When God *took possession of my heart*
So much that since that hour,

19. *Sacra tridentina synodus* (20 December 1905); Latin text DS 3375-3383
20. L 191 [10.1.1904]/ Works 2:144/ OeuvC 222-223
21. NI 15/ Works 1:183-184/ OeuvC 199-200, 907-908
22. Works 2:269, n 7
23. L 4- (1.1.1899 and 31.12.1899) OeuvC 222-223
24. P 47/OeuvC 958-959

Since this *mysterious colloquy*
This divine and delightful *meeting*,
I desire only *to give my life*
To give something of *his great love*
To the beloved in the Eucharist
Who *reposes in* my weak heart,
Flooding it with all his favours.
You recall dear Jesus
Those pure and joyous tears
Which flowed with such gentleness
To your divine feet and on your Heart?
A blessed day, the most beautiful of my life,
A day when *Jesus reposed* in me,
A day on which I *heard his voice*
In the depth of my *ravished* soul.
A happy day, the first glimpse
Of my soul with the God of love,
A foretaste of the heavenly dwelling;
With joy I salute this day

Several people including her mother attest those continuous tears of Elizabeth during Mass and after communion.[25] These verses, not perhaps the greatest of poetry, show the profound spirituality that Elizabeth enjoyed, even before her entry to Carmel.

In these years she frequently reflected on the eucharist in poems as well as retreat notes. As we shall see many of her key insights were already present before she entered Carmel, especially on the connection between the eucharist and suffering.[26] We take up seven themes: adoration, continuing communion, union, suffering, reparation, praise of glory and the communion of saints. We can take for granted common insights such as the eucharist being a source of strength, such as her letter to her mother: 'I am so glad that you are receiving communion more often. It is there, my little Mama, that you will find strength.'[27]

25. OeuvC 959, n 5
26. P 55/OeuvC 967-969
27. L 87/Works 2:12

Eucharistic adoration

Elizabeth has a profound love for eucharistic adoration. She spends most of Sundays in the presence of the blessed sacrament.[28] It is a foretaste of heaven:

> When the Blessed Sacrament is exposed in the chapel, the large grille is open and, so people on the outside can't see us, we are in complete darkness. When I open the door to go in, it seems to me that it is heaven I am entering, and it really is just that in reality, since the One I adore in faith is the same One the glorified contemplate face to face.[29]

The blinds were drawn on the windows so that the sisters in the dark with the grille curtain open would not be seen by anyone in the oratory.

Writing about communion, she echoes Thérèse: 'It is so good to think that after communion we possess all of heaven within our soul except the vision.'[30] She had a similar thought about her cell in the convent: 'If you knew how nice it is in this little cell … Ah, you see, Carmel is not yet heaven, nor is it still earth.'[31]

Union

A key to Elizabeth's understanding of the eucharist is that of union.[32] Several times we have her asking priests to consecrate her along with the host or the chalice. We find it several times in letters to Canon Angles with whom some of her most profound thoughts were shared; it was to him that she had first confided the secret of her vocation.[33]

---

28. E.g. L. 239/Works 2:214 et passim; New Year's Day L 256 /Works 2:238 (to Canon Angles, end Dec 1905). See also L 111/Works 2:43 (to Canon Angeles 7.4.1902)
29. L 137/Works 2:67 (to her aunt Francine Rolland 14.9.1902)
30. L 87 Works /2:12, for echo of Thérèse see Works 2:14, n 3 (here she echoes Thérèse see 2:14, n 3)
31. L 90/Works 2:18 (to her Rolland aunts, 30.8.1901)
32. For her eucharistic teaching see H. U. von Balthasar, *Two Sisters in the Spirit: Thérèse of Lisieux and Elizabeth of the Trinity*, San Francisco, Ignatius, 1992, 373-496 passim, esp 433-434; Sicari, *Elizabetta* 251-265.
33. See L 91, n 1/Works 2:21

I ask you as a child of her father, to please consecrate me at Holy Mass as a sacrifice of praise to the glory of God. Oh, consecrate me so completely that I may be no longer myself but him (see Gal 2:20), so the Father looking at me, may recognise him; so that 'I might be like him in his death,' (Phil 3:10) so that I may suffer in myself what is wanting in his passion for his body the church (Col 1:24), and then bathe me in the Blood of Christ so that I may be strong with his strength; I feel so little, so weak.[34]

Earlier she had written:

No matter what, let us constantly communicate with this Word made flesh, with Jesus who lives in us and wishes to tell us the whole secret.[35]

Speaking of the joy she used to have in celebrating her mother's feast day, she goes on 'I have sacrificed all that on the altar of my heart to him who is a Spouse of blood. It would be very far from the truth to say this cost me nothing, and sometimes I wonder how I was able to leave so good a Mama.'[36] In her last months a

---

34. L. 294 (July 1906) Eng Tr 2:299; see also L 177/2:123 to Canon Angles ca. 27.8.1903; L 244 to Abbé Chevignard 2: 224 (8 Oct 1905) 'would you consecrate me with Him, 'as a sacrifice of praise to his glory,' so that all my aspirations, all my impulses, all my actions may be a homage rendered to his holiness.' To Canon Angles, 'When you consecrate the host in which Jesus becomes incarnate, would you also consecrate your little child to All Powerful Love, so than he may transform her "into a praise of glory". It does me so much good to think that I am going to be given, surrendered, through you! (L 256/2:239 end Dec, 1905); 'I know that you are praying for me every day at Holy Mass. Oh, won't you please place me in the chalice so that my soul may be wholly bathed in this Blood of my Christ for which I so thirst! So as to be wholly pure, wholly transparent, so that the Trinity may be reflected in me as in a crystal. The Trinity so loves to contemplate its beauty in a soul; this draws it to give even more, to come with greater fullness so as to bring about the great mystery of love and unity. L. 131/Works 2:58.To canon Angles.
35. (L 145/Works 2:76-77). See also J. Lafrance, *Apprendre à prier avec Elizabeth de la Trinité* 68-74 – her prayer was loving attention.
36. L 145/Works 2:76-77; L 236/2:210 to her mother; see also P 115, 'I plunge into the infinite.' OeuvC 1057.

sacrificial and eucharistic spirituality deepened in her.[37] For example:

> How I love the thought by St Paul that you sent me! It seems
> to me that it is being realised in me, on this little bed that is
> the altar on which I am being immolated to love. […] If you
> knew what a work of destruction I feel throughout my whole
> being; the road to Calvary has opened, and I am quite joyful
> to walk it like a bride beside the divine Crucified. I will be
> twenty-six on the 18th.[38]

An extended commentary on the need of death to selfishness
and pride, here 'the work of destruction,' can be found in
Elizabeth's treatise to a friend written a few months before her
death; in English it is called *The Greatness of Our Vocation*.[39] Here
'sacrifice of praise' is united with 'praise of glory' for the first
time.

Continuing communion
Balthasar gives a chain of quotations that summarise her
thought on presence:

> 'Let us make a continual holy communion out of our days!'
> (L 172) 'Life in Carmel is communion with God from morn-
> ing to evening, from evening to morning. If he did not fill our
> cells and halls, how empty everything would be.'(L 158). It is
> a 'communion with the soul of the Lord, a conforming to all
> his motions.'[40]

The idea of the communion presence remaining is frequent.
Thus to a first communicant:

> You will come and see me and on that day I will be able to

37. De Meester 2:258, see L 294/2:298-299 to Canon Angles 8 or 9 July
1905
38. Similar thought in L 271/2:267 to Canon Angles: 'I surrender myself
to him so he can do whatever he wants in me. Since you are his priest, oh,
consecrate me to him like a little a little sacrifice of praise who wants to
glorify him in heaven, or on earth with as much suffering as he wishes.'
[trs emended]; DR 18/Works 1:149.
39. GV 3-7/Works 1:125-126
40. *Two Sisters* 433.

open the curtain for you and read in the eyes of my little Berthe all the joy that Jesus has left. More than that, it will be he himself I will see in the dear communicant, for it is not for only a few moments that he comes to her, but in order to remain with her always; remember that well. And when the beautiful day is over, tell yourself that it is not ended, but a union has begun between Jesus and his little communicant that is to be a foretaste of heaven.[41]

In her earlier writings she noted that when she is deprived of actual communion through sickness, the Lord comes to her.[42] Later she wrote to Germaine de Gemeaux:

You are deprived of receiving Him as often as you wish, and I understand your sacrifice so well. But remember that His love does not need a sacrament to come to His little Germaine: communicate with Him the whole day since he is living in your soul.[43]

In Elizabeth two ideas are profoundly interwoven: eucharistic presence and the indwelling of the Trinity.[44] She writes to her sister Guite about having music on the feast of the Sacred Heart: she has it all set up for her sister to arrange: Guite will sing a solo, three other friends are co-opted. Then she writes about the fusion of their two souls in Jesus:

Continue to live in communion with the Three through everything, that is the centre where we meet. I love you very much, my Guite; my communion on Sunday will be for you,

---

41. L 112/Works 2:44 (to Berth Guémard whose sister was a godchild of Elizabeth, 22.0419.02)
42. She had fluid on her knee. L. 62/OeuvC 312
43. L 136/Works 2:65 (14.9.1902)
44. See L 136 to Germaine de Gemeuax Works 2:65 (14.9.1902): 'I will receive Holy Communion for you on that day [17th, her birthday], and if you'd really like to give me your soul, I will consecrate it to the Holy Trinity so that it may introduce you to the depths of the mystery, and so that those Three whom we both love so much may truly be the Centre in which our life passes! […] communicate with him the whole day since he is living in your soul.'

then I'll spend all the day in choir and you'll be there with me. Isn't it good to be close to him? You see, he is my Infinite, in him I love, and am loved, and have everything. A close and profound union.[45]

The two ideas are presented in a striking way in a letter to her mother:

God is spirit and we approach him through faith. Realise that your soul is a temple of God; it is again St Paul who says this; at every moment of the day and night the three Divine Persons are living within you. You do not possess the Sacred Humanity as you do when you receive communion; but the Divinity, that essence the blessed adore in heaven, is in your soul; there is a wholly adorable divine intimacy when you realise that; you are never alone again! If you prefer to think that God is close to you rather than within you, follow your attraction, as long as you live with him. [...] Think that you are with him and act as you would with someone you love; its so simple, there is no need for beautiful thoughts, only an outpouring of your heart.[46]

Three other texts are important for her teaching on the divine indwelling. In the same letter she observes:

I am asking the Holy Spirit to show you this presence of God within you that I spoke to you about. I have looked over some books for you to discuss this, but I would rather see you again before giving them to you. You can believe my

45. L 117/Works 2:46 (to Guite 30.5.1902); a similar text to Germaine de Gemeaux who harboured thoughts of being a Carmelite: 'Always love prayer, dear little Germaine, and when I say prayer, I do not mean so much imposing on yourself a lot of vocal prayers to be said each day as the elevation of the souls towards God through all things that establishes us in a kind of continual communion with the Holy Trinity by quite simply doing everything in Their presence' (L 252/works 2:252) and a few weeks later she writes: 'I am keeping my rendez-vous with you in the mystery of the Three, pray for your Sabeth who loves you very much and feels her soul to be very close to yours.' (L 119/Works 2:48, ca. June 15, 1902). See also L 172/Works 2:116; L 186/Works 2:137 to an expectant mother.
46. L 273/Works 2:271 (about May 1906)

doctrine, for it is not mine. [...] Realise that your soul is the temple of God, it is again Saint Paul who says this. [See 1 Cor 3:16-17; 2 Cor 6:16] At every moment of the day and night.[47]

In another text she again writes to her mother about the divine presence:

> Yes, little Mama, take advantage of your solitude to recollect yourself with God; while your body is resting, think how he is the rest of your soul and how, just as a child loves to remain in the arms of her mother, you may find rest in the arms of this God who surrounds you on all sides.[48]

Writing to Mde Angle, a sister-in-law of the Canon, who was suffering desolation, she says:

> I am going to give you my 'secret': think about this God who dwells in you, whose temple you are (1 Cor 3:16). St Paul speaks about this and we can believe him. Little by little, the soul gets used to living in his sweet company, it understands that it is carrying within it a little heaven where the God of love has fixed his home. Do not say that this is not for you ...[49]

Elizabeth wrote thirteen letters to the Abbé André Chevignard, then a seminarian; he was the brother of Elizabeth's brother-in-law. This correspondence, which would remind one of Thérèse's to her two missionary 'brothers', develops the main themes of Elizabeth's spirituality.[50] She writes on remaining at the Lord's feet:

> Don't you find that in action, when we are in Martha's role, the soul can remain wholly adoring, buried like Magdalene in her contemplation, staying by this source (Fr *source*) like someone who is starving; and this is how I understand the Carmelite's apostolate as well as the priest's. Then both can radiate God, give him to souls, if they constantly stay close to

---

47. L 273/Works 2:270-271
48. L 301/2:311 (about 26.7.1906)
49. L 249/2:230, ca. 26.11.05
50. See R. Girardello, ed, *Amati fratelli: Lettere ai sacerdoti – S. Teresa di Gesù Bambino B. Elizabetta della Trinità*, Rome, Ed. OCD, 1997

this divine source. It seems to me that we should draw so close to the Master, in such communion with his soul, to identify ourselves with all its movements, and then go out as he did, according to the will of the Father. Then it does not matter what happens to the soul, since it has faith in the One it loves who dwells in it.[51]

Here we see other classical themes of the French school of spirituality in addition to the 'God Alone' noted earlier. The emphasis on priesthood is Carmelite but also French. Particularly important for the French school of spirituality is the prominence of the incarnation and of entering into the states of life and feeling of the Lord. This school goes back to Cardinal Bérulle (d. 1629), who it should be remembered brought the discalced Carmelite nuns from Spain to France (1604). Dijon, a year later, was in fact the third foundation in France and it had for a time as prioress the companion of St Teresa of Avila, the Venerable Mother Anne of Jesus.[52]

Elizabeth had a profound love of eucharistic adoration. The eucharist is a foretaste of heaven; the One in heaven and the One adored in the host are one:

It seems to me that nothing better expresses the love in God's heart than the eucharist: it is union, consummation, he in us, we in him, isn't that heaven on earth? Heaven in faith while awaiting the face-to-face vision that we so desire. [...] During the whole Octave [of Corpus Christi] we have the blessed sacrament exposed in the oratory; these are divine hours spent in this little corner of heaven where we possess the vision in substance under the humble host. Yes, he whom the blessed contemplate in light and we adore in faith is really the same One. The other day someone wrote to me a beauti-

51. L 158/Works 2:96 (24.3.1903). See DR 20/Works 1:150 on continual adoration arising from being rooted and grounded in love (see Eph 3:16-17)
52. It would be interesting to see what books were in the library of Dijon at the time of Elizabeth. The nuns from Dijon were dispersed at the time of the French revolution, but Dijon was refounded in 1866.

ful thought; I send it on to you: 'Faith is the face-to-face in darkness.'[53]

Eucharist and Suffering

The views of the saints about suffering are likely to make us uneasy. What normal person would want suffering, much less see it as a joy? Elizabeth often speaks about suffering, frequently in a eucharistic context.[54] We can find a general statement from her last year:

> Each incident, each event and each suffering, as well as each joy, is a sacrament that gives us joy and the soul can no longer distinguish among these things, rather she passes beyond them to repose above all in the Lord himself.[55]

She had quite frightful pain in her final illness. Indeed she remarked: 'I'm suffering so much that I now can understand suicide.'[56] She speaks of being offered as a victim, of her bed of pain being an altar.[57] In this time of deep suffering she delights to visit a gallery (*tribune*), an area that looked out on to the oratory:

> My little legs are making progress, and I am taking advantage of it to make visits to the little tribune, it's divine! I am God's little recluse, and when I return to my dear cell to continue there the conversation begun at the tribune, a divine joy

53. L 165/Works 2:105. (To Abbé Chevignard 14.619.03)

54. See J. Moorcroft, *He Is My Heaven: the Life of Elizabeth of the Trinity*, Washington, ACS, 2001, 113-142; C. De Meester, *Elizabeth de la Trinité racontrée par elle-même*, Paris, Cerf, 2002, 85-111; Giovanna della Croce, *Elizabetta della Trinità: Una vita di lode di Dio*, Milan, Paoline, 1993, 67-77; R. Moretti, *Introduzione a Elizabetta della Trinità: Vita scritti dottrina*, Rome, Postulazione Gen OCD, 1984, 177-180; Sicari, *Elizabetta* 225-250; P.A. Févotte, *Aimer la bible avec Elizabeth de la Trinité*, Paris, Cerf, 1991, 73-86. The work of J. de Bono, *Elizabetta de la Trinità*, Vatican, 2002, came to hand too late to be considered.

55. CF 10/Works 1:97; see also L 264 /2:252: 'Look at every suffering as well as every joy as coming directly from him, and then your life will be a continual communion, since everything will be like a sacrament that will give God to you.' See Works 1:134-135; GV 6/Works 1:126 – 'What delightful peace we experience when we place our joy in suffering.'

56. See Works 2:353, 2 at L 329

57. For references see Works 2:230, n 1

takes hold of me; I so love solitude with him alone, and I lead a simple hermit's life that is truly delightful. You know, it is far from being exempt from helplessness; I, too, need to seek my Master who hides himself well; but then I stir up my faith, and I am happier at not enjoying his presence so I can make him enjoy my love. At night, when you awake, unite yourself to me. I wish I could invite you here near me; it is so mysterious, so silent, this little cell with its white walls that set off a black wooden cross without a Corpus. It is mine, the place where I must immolate myself at every moment to be conformed to my crucified Bridegroom. Saint Paul said: 'What I want is to know him, Christ, to share his sufferings, so as to become like him in his death.' By this is understood that mystical death by which the soul annihilates itself and forgets itself so completely that it goes to die in God in order to be transformed in him.[58]

We find elsewhere the idea that the eucharist effects transformation.[59]

Writing to her mother, who is undergoing some trials, Elizabeth tells her that suffering is purifying:

I can't tell you how much I am praying for you, for you see, I am jealous for the beauty of your soul; I feel He wants it for His own and all the trials He is making you pass through have been sent only for that.[60]

The complex attitude of Elizabeth to suffering can be deduced from two texts from late in her life:

I cannot say that I love suffering in itself; but I love it because it conforms me to him who is my Bridegroom and my Love. Oh, you see, [suffering] bestows such sweet peace, such profound joy on the soul, and you end up putting your happiness in everything that is irritating. Little Mama, try to put joy – not the joy you can feel but the joy of your will – into every irritation, every sacrifice, and say to the Master: 'I am

58. L 298 / Works 2:305-306 (to her sister 16.7.1906)
59. CF 18 / Works 1:100
60. L 301 / Works 2:311 (26.7.1906); see also L 314 / Works 2:332

not worthy to suffer that for you, I do not deserve that con-
formity with you.' You'll see that my recipe is excellent; it
puts a delightful peace in the depths of the heart and draws
you closer to God.[61]

And:

I do not forget you, I assure you, on my cross where I taste
unknown joys. I understand that suffering is the revelation of
Love, and I rush to it; it is my beloved dwelling place where I
find peace and rest, where I am sure to meet my Master and
dwell with him.[62]

We will never understand the mystics unless we keep in mind
that they are madly, crazily in love with God who has transformed them totally. They can find meaning and peace in suffering. We may not have the same openness to suffering as the
mystics, but when suffering comes our way, as it inevitably will,
we can find in the mystics an approach that may help to sustain
us. The mystic's view of the cross is not in any way to reject or
lessen palliative care and hospice or other nursing. It is in offering us an attitude that the mystics can serve our world which is
often in denial about sin, evil, pain and suffering. There is a saying in Alcoholics Anonymous circles: 'You may not be able to
change your situation; you can change your attitude.' Elizabeth's
view of suffering, especially in a eucharistic framework, is pot-
entially of the greatest value as we struggle with the mystery of
suffering.

Reparation

The theme of reparation is found throughout the compass of
Elizabeth's writings. She loves the forty hours adoration.

We had the Blessed Sacrament exposed for forty hours, and it

<hr/>

61. L 317/Works 2:338 (to her mother September 1906). In October 1906
she would write to her mother, '...you draw down on me graces of
strength for suffering, which I love more and more and which my
Master does not spare me.' L 325/Works 2:348
62. L 323/Works 2:344-345 (to Mde de Sourdon grieving for her sister,
9.10.1906)

was very good to come to console him. It's even so good that
you would like to stay forever, don't you agree?[63]

The forty hours devotion had begun in Milan in the mid sixteenth century. In time it would rise to perpetual exposition and
to reparation at carnival time before Lent.

> During these days of forty hours, we have the Blessed
> Sacrament exposed in our dear oratory. Today, Sunday, I
> spent nearly my whole day close to him, and I so wished that,
> by means of my love, I could make him forget all the evil
> being committed during these carnival days.[64]

A poem, *Perpetual Adoration*, written after a retreat and almost
eighteen months before her entry to Carmel, shows that even
then she had a profound and reflected eucharistic spirituality.
Some literally translated lines will give a sense of her religious
experience at the time:

> I love each day to come
> To hear you, to chat with you, to see you ...
> I cannot tell all the delights
> Of these conversations alongside the Saviour ...
> My supreme Love, oh my King,
> Jesus a captive and solitary
> When I am with you,
> I am no longer on earth ...
> When I hear your voice
> O my Spouse, my good Master,
> Who silences all my being,
> I understand and see nothing but you ...
> Near him I am happy,
> He is my Life and my Love.
> I so much desire for him
> Suffering, to suffer always.
> To suffer and console his Heart
> Overwhelmed by so many pains
> To suffer! To prove my love

63. L 108 / Works 2:38 (to her Rolland aunts 11.2.1902)
64. L 194 / Works 2:149 (to Mde Angles 14 or 15.2.19.04)

To Jesus my only Love.[65]

Later in the convent Elizabeth seeks to be constantly in prayer and to be a victim for Jesus. She writes to her sister Guite [Marguerite]: 'Tell him, the One who knows everything, and who is the guest of your soul; realise that he is within you as in a little host.'[66] In these eucharistic texts we may well wonder with De Meester if Elizabeth may be indebted to Thérèse's *Acts of Oblation* which Elizabeth had copied out at least four times.[67]

Several times we find the image of both Jesus and Elizabeth being prisoners in tine oratory and in Carmel: 'I am the prisoner of the divine Prisoner, we are each other's captives.'[68] Thus in the context of assuring her sister Guite of prayers for her wedding, Elizabeth writes:

We will have the Blessed Sacrament in the chapel that day, and while the church consecrates your union, the Carmelite, the happy one chained by Christ, will spend the day at his feet becoming wholly praying, wholly adoring, for these 'two' whom God wishes to be 'one!' [...] I had a very holy visit in the parlour with Abbé Chevignard; I believe that there has been a *fusion* between the soul of the priest and that of the Carmelite.[69]

Again:

Every Sunday we have the Blessed Sacrament exposed in the oratory. When I open the door and contemplate the divine Prisoner who made me a prisoner in this dear Carmel, it seems that it is almost the gate to heaven that is opening! Then I place before my Jesus all those who are in my heart,

65. P. 67/OeuvC 982-984; compare J 5-10/OeuvC 810-815 from the same days in early February 1899
66. L 93/Works 2:23 (12.919.01)
67. See Works 2:24, n. 2. Also 'Remain in me as in a tabernacle, and never separate yourself from your little victim.' (*hostie* can mean 'victim' and 'host')
68. L 198/Works 2:155; L 209/Works 2:169
69. L 135/Works 2:64 (to her sister before some days before marriage on 14 Sept 1902). The marriage was to Georges Chevignard whose brother l'Abbé André was in frequent correspondence with Elizabeth.

and there, close to him I find them again. You see that I think
of you very often, and I know that you do not forget me, that
every morning when you offer the Holy Sacrifice you remember your little Carmelite who confided her secret to you
a very long time ago.[70]

She frequently returns to this scene of darkness and light:

I had a delightful, divine Shrovetide. Monday and Tuesday
we had the Blessed Sacrament in the oratory and on Sunday
in the choir; I spent nearly the whole day close to him, and
my Guite was there with me, for it seems to me that I kept her
in my soul. It was very nice, I assure you. We were in darkness for the grille was open, and all the light came from him. I
so love to see the great grille between us: he is a prisoner for
me, and I am a prisoner for him![71]

Praise of Glory and Eucharist

'Praise of glory' is a phrase indissolubly associated with
Elizabeth.[72] In January 25 1904 she first used it in a letter to Abbé
Chevignard.[73] She then develops it as being consecrated as a little sacrifice of praise.[74] In a letter to Canon Angles it has eucharistic overtones: she wishes to be consecrated as a praise of
glory through the Mass.[75]

70. L 91/Works 2:20 (to Canon Angles 11.9.1901); Canon Emilien
Isidore Angles, then 66 was curé at Saint Hilaire where the Catez family
regularly visited him.
71. L 109/Works 2:40 with note on grille 41, n.6
72. See Sicari, *Elizabetta* 251-265; L. Boriello, *Spiritual Doctrine of Blessed
Elizabeth of the Trinity: Apostolic Contemplative*, New York, Alba, 1986,
103-118; CF 41-44/Works 1:111-113
73. L 191/Works 2:144-145; see DR 17/Works 149
74. L. 271/Works 2:267 (to Canon Angles 9.5.1906). Writing to the Abbé
Chevignon a year earlier: 'When you consecrate the host, in which
Jesus, 'who alone is the Holy One,' is about to become incarnate, would
you consecrate me with him, 'as a sacrifice of praise to his glory' so that
all my aspirations, all my impulses, all my actions may be a homage
rendered to his Holiness.' L. 244/Works 2:224.
75. L 271/Works 2:267 (9.5.1906); see L 294/Works 2:299 (to Canon
Angles 8/9.7. 1906). See J 151, 156 OeuvC 886-887 with notes 149 and
157 for similarities with Thérèse.

A dense letter to Abbé Chevignard reflecting on 'our conversation is in heaven' (Phil 3:20), she writes:

Let us ask him to make us true in our love, to make us sacrificial beings, for it seems to me that sacrifice is only love put into action [...] I love this thought, that the life of the priest (and of the Carmelite) is an Advent that prepares for the incarnation in souls. [...] On December 8th (since you are a high priest), would you consecrate me to the power of his love so I may in truth be 'Laudem (sic) gloriae,' I read in St Paul that it was my vocation even now in exile while awaiting the eternal Sanctus.[76]

The Praise of Glory sums up her earlier more tentative experiences of belonging and of union: 'I feel as if all the treasures of the soul of Christ belong to me.'[77]

Communion of saints

Like St Thérèse, her Lisieux sister, Elizabeth had a profound sense of the Communion of Saints. She felt that she shared in the good things of God on earth with others and she shared in the life of those in glory. She writes to a missionary to China with the Lazarists, the Abbé Henri-Joseph Beaubis:

It seems to me that the souls on earth and those glorified in the light of vision are so close to each other, since they are all in communion with the same God, the same Father, who gives himself to the former in faith and mystery, and satisfies the others in his divine light ... But he is the Same One, and we carry him within us. He bends over us with all his charity, day and night, wanting to communicate with us, to infuse us with his divine life, so as to make us deified beings who radiate him everywhere. [...] I am praying fervently for you, that God may invade all the powers of your soul, that he may make you live in communion with his whole majesty, that every thing in you may be divine and marked with his seal,

---

76. L 250/Works 2:233 . 29.11.05 (this is the first time to use Latin *Laudem gloriae*)

77. L 91/Works 2:20 (to Canon Angles 11.9.1901)

so that you may be another Christ working for the glory of
the Father. [...] Let us be wholly his, Monsieur l'Abbé, let us
be flooded with his divine essence, that he may be the Life of
our soul, that we may consciously remain night and day
under his divine action. [...] Thanks for your kind letter. Yes,
may God unite our souls in him for his glory. Union, communion...[78]

The communion of saints is a concrete reality for her, especially
through the eucharist:

I no longer go to see her or her dear mama whom I love so
much, but I keep a rendez-vous with them near the tabernacle: when they think of me they should go there, they will
always find me close to God; let him be our rendez-vous,
shall we, Cécile? If he came this morning into your little
heart, it was not to pass through it and go away, but to remain there always; keep him well, my darling, and keep me
also in that dear sanctuary.[79]

In a letter to a lady who asked her to try to get in contact with a
dead relative, Elizabeth wrote powerfully about the communion
of saints, observing that 'I am closer to the dead than to the living', adding:

You ask me to get in contact with her ... Oh, if you knew how
we live by faith in Carmel, how imagination and feeling are
excluded from our relationship with God ... I was astonished
that you would say that to me, but I thought that I might
have misinterpreted the meaning of your words. Oh, yes,
very willingly I unite myself with the dear deceased. I enter
into communion with her, I find her once more in him by
whom she lives: and so each time I draw near to God, faith
tells me that I am already drawing close to her.[80]

Here union with God is a means of spiritual communication.

---

78. L 124/2:53-54 (22. 06.1902); see also DR 20/Works 1:150
79. L 116/Works 2:46 (to Cecile Lignon, 29.5.1902
80. L 323 /Works. 2:344 to Mde Sourdon on the death of her sister (9.10.
1906)

One might ask if this closeness through the eucharist to those who are departed might not be an answer for people who otherwise might seek contact in séances or in African magic or spirit rituals. In Jesus all are alive, and through him and the Virgin Mary we can have significant communication with the deceased and forge bonds with them of forgiveness, love, thanks etc. What we may not have said in life can be communicated to them through Jesus in holy communion.

She wrote to her sister commenting on their father's anniversary:

> On October 2nd we will be united very specially to pray for our dear Papa. You see, I think he is so happy when he looks down from heaven on his little one in Carmel. Even since I have been here I have felt much closer to him.[81]

A typical expression of her concrete experience of being in the communion of saints can be found in yet another letter to her wise guide, Canon Angles:

> So I live in thanksgiving, uniting myself to the eternal praise, that is being sung in the heaven of the saints; I am making my apprenticeship down here! [...] Pray for your little child, too, consecrate her with the sacred host so that nothing of poor Elizabeth remains but so that she may be wholly of the Trinity.[82]

Conclusion

What are we to make of Elizabeth's eucharistic teaching today? She was able to spend long hours, the most of each Sunday, in eucharistic adoration. Such protracted prayer is not possible for most of us. Is it therefore beyond us? One could answer that Elizabeth has charted out the mysterious depths of the eucharist; she has mapped out a journey into mystery. We may not travel to where she arrived, but we can see her experience as a guide, a

---

81. There is no explicit eucharistic reference; see also writing to Mde de Sourdon on the tenth anniversary of her husband's death (L 223 / Works 2:191) where Elizabeth speaks of feeling close to him.
82. L 225 / 2:195 (sometime before 8.3 1905)

chart in our own journey. Her life can touch the deepest areas of
our hearts and allow them to be drawn by divine love into a response and reverence for the beauty of the love Jesus has revealed in the eucharist.

We end with comments from Hans Urs von Balthasar, one of
her first, and in some ways still among her finest interpreters:

> A number of elements, harmoniously integrated, were long
> present in Elizabeth's consciousness: Carmel's apostolic con-
> templation, the inclination of the entire spirit towards eternity,
> the presence of God in the soul, love for the crucified and eu-
> charistic Lord and the deeply felt yet still abstract idea of
> God's triunity, sketched out in the name of this love, love for
> the holy scripture, especially for Paul and his letters. All
> these were present but had not yet crystallised around the
> one enfolding and unfolding centre.[83]

Then with the discovery of the 'Praise of Glory' in January 1904
all would be united:

> Adoration filled her to the limit with the mystery she con-
> templated: the indisputable present-ness of God, before her
> and in her, in the nakedness, surrender and self-sacrifice of
> eternal love. Nothing but contemplation and awe ... And this
> astonishing silence is heaven on earth. In it, presence not
> bliss makes a down payment on an eternal heaven in which
> bliss will be found simply in the repeated and everlasting
> wonder of presence.[84]

---

83. *Two Sisters* 385
84. Ibid, 440

CHAPTER FOUR

The Eucharist and St Teresa of Avila

Philip McParland ODC
in conversation with Eltin Griffin O Carm

E.G. What is your deepest conviction as a Carmelite about Teresa of Avila?

McP I am convinced that Teresa of Avila was one of the greatest women in the history of the church. There have been many great women in every generation whose wisdom we inherit. Among the wisdom figures it would be difficult to choose say between Teresa and Catherine of Siena. I am influenced by the fact that Pope Paul VI declared them both Doctors of the Church on the same day in 1970, the first women ever to be given such a signal honour. Both women were mystics with their feet on the ground, very much in touch with nature, with the world around them, with the political scene and with what was taking place in the church. Worlds apart you could say. Catherine lived in the fourteenth century, a period of schism in the church, the Pope living in Avignon. Catherine dared to speak out even to the point of challenging the Pope. Teresa, living in sixteenth century Spain, was forced to be more circumspect. Living at the time of the Inquisition, when all writing about prayer was a dangerous occupation, less gifted persons than Teresa were suddenly seized by the servants of the Inquisition and found themselves in prison.

E.G. What would you say is common to both women?

McP I would venture to say what John Paul II in his encyclical *Novo Millenio Inuente (At the beginning of a New Millennium*

2002) describes as the lived theology of the saints. Catherine was an unlettered person who, we are told, learned to read only in her teens. Teresa had been an avid reader all her life. Both would have garnered that lived theology not so much from formal study but from attentive listening to sermons, from spiritual guidance, from the liturgy itself and from their own mystical experience of the Christian mysteries. As Paul VI stated in 1970, 'lucid and profound in absorption of the divine truths and mysteries of the faith'.

E.G.   To get to the living theology of Teresa, especially in the area of the eucharist, you might give a brief sketch of her life.

McP   Teresa was born in Avila in 1515 and died in Torremolinos in 1582. At the age of twenty she entered the local Carmelite Convent of the Incarnation in Avila, which housed a very large community of over one hundred nuns. She struggled to live her life as best she could. The sheer size of the community was a big obstacle in her search for solitary prayer. More so the comings and goings within the monastery. There was a lot of parlour activity. Benefactors from the city were very demanding, wanting to spend time with members of the community in the parlours. Teresa, because of her attractive and warm personality, was often sent for. In the end she made what was a very bold move. She had the courage to abandon the Convent of the Incarnation and founded the smaller Convent of St Joseph in the same city. Thus began the reform of the Carmelite Order in Spain, which in turn was to lead to the establishment of what came to be known as the Discalced Carmelites.

E.G.   What was her motivation in plunging into this new venture?

McP   Unlike the Convent of the Incarnation, she wanted her

communities to be small, say fourteen, fifteen, sixteen in number. She wanted to create a lifestyle for her sisters which would enable them to be faithful to prayer, especially silent prayer, not excluding, of course, liturgical prayer. Allied with provision for prayer she wanted the sisters to have quality community life, which was well nigh impossible in the Convent of the Incarnation. The ideal for her was a more simple lifestyle. Between the year 1558, when she was 43, and the year 1582 in which she died, she founded 17 convents in Spain. Some going for a mystic!

E.G.   What kind of a woman was Teresa? How would you describe her personality?

McP   She was naturally gifted, a woman with a very lively disposition and a born organiser. Practical and witty, she had a great gift of friendship, an outstanding woman by any standard. She was a consummate teacher especially in the art of prayer, drawing mainly on her own experience. All contemporary accounts describe her as a fine looking woman with a tendency towards plumpness, sparkling black eyes, expressive white hands always in motion. There was a magnanimity about Teresa that invited confidence. Physically big as she was, she had a heart to match; a very human person who is recorded as saying 'God preserve us from sour faced saints.'

E.G.   To get to her approach to the eucharist and how she lived it out.

McP   She was very focused on one particular aspect of the eucharist, Christ's presence in what she called the blessed sacrament. To put this in context I might recall what the Second Vatican Council stated about the presence or rather the presences of Christ in the eucharist. In the Vatican II approach, the eucharist is an encounter with the living Christ, crucified and risen. It goes on to say that Christ is present in four different ways.

Firstly, he is present in the community. 'For where two or three are gathered in my name, I am there in the middle of them.' (Mk 18:20) When we come to celebrate the eucharist we encounter Jesus in each other because we are his brothers and sisters. We are his Body and we mediate to each other the presence of Christ.

Secondly, Christ is present in the person of the priest. The priest acts 'in persona Christi'. He takes the place of Christ. He presides over the people who come together. He prays with them and on their behalf. He breaks the word for the assembled people. He breaks the word and he breaks the bread. That is his special role.

Thirdly, Christ is present in the scriptures. As the *General Instruction of the Roman Missal* puts it 'When the scriptures are read in the church God himself speaks to his people and it is Christ present in his word who proclaims the gospel.' (No 9)

Lastly, Christ is present in the bread and in the wine. The bread and wine of the eucharist are described as the bread of life and the cup of eternal salvation. Christ is present in a way that surpasses all other forms of his presence. In traditional and familiar language, Christ is present in the blessed sacrament. It is this presence of Christ in the eucharist, which is the focus for Teresa and also the focus for her teaching. That is what I want to dwell on now. She doesn't seem to say an awful lot about the other three presences. She concentrates upon Christ's presence in the blessed sacrament. This was the focus of her devotion and equally the focus of her teaching.

E.G.   She focused on the presence of Christ?

McP   Teresa focused on the presence of Christ in the blessed sacrament and for the following reasons, principally because of the denial of the real presence by the Protestant Reformers. These were difficult and painful times in the life of the church and, even though the Reformation had little or no impact in Spain, Teresa was aware of what was happening in other parts of Europe. It was a great cause of confusion for her that the presence of Christ in the blessed sacrament was being questioned and even denied. She leaves us in no doubt as to how she felt about the reformers, 'those heretics' as she called them. She did not put a tooth in it.

E.G.   What did Teresa herself then believe about the real presence?

McP   Maybe the best way to answer your question is to give you a flavour of her teaching, to let Teresa speak in her own words. Let me begin with this. This is the way she understood the presence of Christ in the blessed sacrament, what we call the real presence. This is what she writes in *The Way of Perfection* (34:8):

> 'If we don't want to be fools and blind the intellect there is no reason for doubt. Receiving communion is not like picturing with the imagination, as when we reflect upon the Lord on the cross or in other episodes of the passion, when we picture within ourselves how things happened to him in the past. In communion the event is happening now, and it is entirely true. There is no reason to go looking for him in some other place farther away.'

And in a further section of the same work she writes:

> 'I know that for many years, when she received communion, this person, though she was not very perfect, strove to strengthen her faith so that in receiving her Lord it was as if, with her bodily eyes, she saw him enter her house. Since she believed that this Lord truly entered her poor home, she freed herself from all exterior things when it was possible and entered to be with him. She strove to recollect the senses so that all

of them would take notice of so great a good; I mean
that they would not impede the soul from recognising
it. She considered she was at his feet and wept with the
Magdalene, no more nor less than if she were seeing
him with her bodily eyes in the house of the Pharisee.
And even though she didn't feel devotion, faith told
her that he was indeed there.' (*Way* 34:7)

And in a section from the *Life* she puts in this way:

'When I approached to receive communion and recalled that extraordinary majesty I had seen and considered that it was present in the blessed sacrament
(and the Lord often desires that I behold it in the host),
my hair stood on end; the whole experience seemed to
annihilate me.' (*Life* 38:19)

Another reason why Teresa focused on the presence of
Christ in the blessed sacrament was because of her desire
to have the blessed sacrament reserved in the new monas-
teries of the Reform. When she founded a new monastery
what gave her deep satisfaction was that this would be
another place where the blessed sacrament would be reserved. Teresa had two simple criteria for discerning
whether or not a new monastery should be founded in a
new location. One was would the sisters have the daily
eucharist, and the other criterion was would they have
enough means to support themselves. The third reason
that I am offering why Teresa focused on the presence of
Christ in the blessed sacrament was because of her own
personal experience. For Teresa personally the presence
of Christ in the blessed sacrament, or to call it, if you like,
holy communion, is the source of three things, a source of
healing, a source of strength and a source of intimacy.

E.G.   Perhaps we do not pay enough attention to the fact that
the eucharist is a source of healing. Contemporary theology sees the eucharist as the sacrament of healing.

McP   Teresa was in no doubt that the presence of Christ in the
       blessed sacrament was a powerful source of healing; spir-
       itual healing, emotional healing, healing of relationships
       and physical healing. This is what she has to say about it.
       She is writing about herself in the following passage:

> 'Do you think this heavenly food fails to provide sus-
> tenance, even for these bodies, that it is not a great
> medicine even for bodily ills? I know it is. I know a
> person with serious illness, who often experiences
> great pain, who through this bread had them taken
> away as though by a gesture of the hand and was
> made completely well. This is a common experience,
> and the illnesses are very recognisable, for I don't
> think they could be feigned. And because the wonders
> this most sacred bread effects in those who worthily
> receive it are well known, I will not mention many that
> could be mentioned regarding this person I've spoken
> of. I was able to know of them, and I know that this is
> no lie. But the Lord had given her such living faith that
> when she heard some persons saying they would have
> liked to have lived at the time Christ our God walked
> in the world, she used to laugh to herself. She won-
> dered what more they wanted since in the most
> blessed sacrament they had him just as truly present as
> he was then.
>
> Now then, if when he went about in the world the
> mere touch of his robes cured the sick, why doubt, if
> we have faith, that miracles will be worked while he is
> within us and that he will give what we ask of him,
> since he is in our house? His Majesty is not accust-
> omed to paying poorly for his lodging if the hospitality
> is good.' (*Way* 34:3)

       It is up to us to provide the hospitality. He will do the rest.

E.G.   Reminds one of Lourdes, does it not?

McP   Yes, very much. So much of the healing at Lourdes takes
      place during the afternoon procession of the blessed
      sacrament, especially when the monstrance is brought
      separately to sick people who are unable to join in the
      procession. As we know, a complete cure does happen on
      occasion at Lourdes but much more common is the grace
      of being healed. For many people the visit to Lourdes can
      have a transforming effect. Some return home with hope
      rekindled, with the assurance that they are loved and that
      their sufferings are worthwhile. The eucharist does play a
      leading part in the healing process.

E.G. To look at the second aspect, a source of strength.

McP   As you know Teresa was a tireless writer. We have al-
      ready quoted from *The Way of Perfection* which she wrote
      for her own nuns. The second part of the *Way* is a com-
      mentary on the Our Father. When she comes to the peti-
      tion 'give us this day our daily bread' she cuts loose in
      terms of her teaching on the eucharist. She interprets that
      petition in this way: the food we need for our bodies, but
      also the food we need to nourish our relationship with
      Christ, the eucharist. In Chapter 34 of *The Way* Teresa tells
      us 'that by the gift of the blessed sacrament Jesus remains
      with us to help, encourage and sustain us in doing God's
      will, that what we had prayed in the previous petition
      might be done in us.' That is interesting, isn't it, that the
      petition after 'thy will be done on earth' reminds us 'as it
      is in heaven' is 'give us this day our daily bread.' And
      later in the same chapter she says that Jesus has given us
      the manna and nourishment of his humanity that we
      might find him and that he is teaching us to set our wills
      on heavenly ways. A very important thing for Teresa was
      the will of God. The goal of her spiritual life was divine
      union. A union of wills reminds us of what St Augustine
      said: 'Love God and do what you will.' If your will and
      God's will become one you will love God. In practical

terms to do the will of God seems to me is to put on the heart and the mind of Christ. It is to live as Christ lived. Teresa was aware of her own weakness. Left to herself, relying on her own strength she knew that it was impossible for her to do the will of God, to live like Christ. It was in the bread of the eucharist, the great source of spiritual nourishment, that she received the strength to be able to do the Lord's will in her life, to live the way of Christ and so to be conformed to Christ. To remind ourselves again of what Vatican II has said about the eucharist: 'the sign of unity and the source of strength.' The reality is that none of us can live the gospel as Jesus would want us to live it without the strength that comes from the food of the eucharist. The way I understand this is that we receive the Body of Christ in the eucharist in order to become the Body of Christ for each other. That is why the priest reminds us at the end of Mass: 'The Mass is ended, go forth now to love and to serve the Lord.' We need the strength that comes from the eucharist to empower us to live the gospel in the reality and in the situations of our daily lives.

E.G.   Show us how contemporary Teresa is in her teaching, the way she applies the eucharist to life. You might elaborate then on the eucharist as the source of intimacy.

McP   Yes, the source of intimacy with Christ, her beloved, her friend, her majesty, her companion, her master, her all. In Chapter 6 of John's gospel Jesus says: 'Whoever eats my flesh and drinks my blood lives in me and I live in that person. As the living Father serves me and I draw life from the Father, so whoever eats me will draw life from me.' Receiving Christ in holy communion was an experience of communion with Christ, a union with Christ. For Teresa the time after communion was a time of intimacy, a time to be with her Lord, her beloved. Teresa had a unique longing to receive holy communion. Let's listen to the way she describes it herself. In the book of her life, she writes:

'On occasion there came over me such ardent desires to receive communion that I don't think they could be exaggerated. They came upon me one morning when it was raining so hard it seemed impossible to leave the house. When I was outside the house, I was already so outside myself with the desire for communion that even should lances have been held to my heart I think I'd have gone into their midst; how much more into the midst of rain.' (*Life* 39:22)

Because of Teresa's great desire to receive Christ in holy communion it is understandable that many of her mystical experiences took place after she received holy communion. Teresa wrote seven short pieces known as 'soliloquies', spontaneous prayers which record her inspirations after receiving holy communion. She also wrote what are called her 'spiritual testimonies' recording the favours given to her upon receiving holy communion. On one occasion Jesus showed her that the soul is filled with the Godhead and she heard the words 'Don't try to hold me within yourself but try to hold yourself within me.' She heard also revealed 'that the soul, after receiving holy communion, detaches itself from everything so as to abide more in me. It is no longer the soul that lives but I.'

After communion her focus was on her relationship with Christ, rather than using the time to intercede for the needs of others. Why? For her it's the time to be with her Lord, to experience his presence, to abide in his love. She writes as follows:

'On another occasion after receiving communion, it seemed most clear to me, she says, that our Lord sat beside me and he began to console me with great favours and he told me among other things, "See me here, daughter, for it is I; give me your hands." And it seemed he took them and placed them on his side and said, "Behold my wounds. You are not without me".' (*Spiritual Testimonies* 12:6).

Just to share something very personal. One of the most significant and vivid memories of my own mother is that of her in prayer after she received holy communion. She was in another world. Her eyes were closed and there was a calm expression on her face and that expression on her face suggested that she was in the presence of someone who possessed her heart. I used to stay behind with her as she knelt in prayer, happy just to be next to her. Observing her wrapped in prayer and also receiving something of the spiritual energy that seemed to come from her. I wonder what it was like to be in the presence of St Teresa of Avila after she received holy communion.

E.G.   Thank you for sharing that with me. I had a similar experience over in England which has stayed in my memory all my life. I was giving a mission in the Parish of SS Mary and John in Wolverhampton. On Sunday morning I celebrated an early Mass at 8.00 am in the Mercy Convent chapel. A Hungarian man came to communion. As he came to receive holy communion his face was aglow. That is the only way I can describe it. He put his whole being into the act of receiving communion and it was as if he were being transformed in body, heart and mind. I love to recall that experience which has always been a challenge to me as I receive holy communion myself.

And a final word, if you would, from Teresa

McP   'Now then, sisters, consider that if in the beginning you do not fare well, the devil will make you think you find more devotion in other things and less in this recollection after communion. Do not abandon this practice; the Lord will see in it how much you love him.' (*Way* 35:2)

* All quotes in this section are taken from *The Collected Works of St Teresa of Avila*, ICS Publications, Washington DC, 1980

CHAPTER FIVE

The Eucharist in St Mary Magdalene de'Pazzi

Míceál O'Neill O Carm

The purpose and ideal of the Carmelite way of life is twofold, according to a text called *The Book of the Institution of the First Monks*, from the fourteenth century:

> One part we acquire by our own effort and the exercise of the virtues, with the help of divine grace. This is to offer God a heart that is holy and pure from all actual stain of sin ... The other goal of this life is granted to us as the free gift of God: namely, not only after death but even in this mortal life, to taste somewhat in the heart and to experience in the mind the power of the divine presence and the sweetness of heavenly glory.[1]

The story of Mary Magdalene de'Pazzi, like that of many Carmelites, is an accomplishment of this ideal. For significant periods in her life she enjoyed encounters with God that gave her a knowledge of him that allows us to see that the offering of a pure heart to God, and the enjoyment in this life of the power of divine presence and the sweetness of heavenly glory, are something very real. In the case of this saint, much of her intimate knowledge of God was connected with her participation in the Mass and her love for the blessed sacrament. The 'blessed sacrament' is the term that she most often uses to refer to what we now more commonly refer to as the eucharist.

Mary Magdalene was born in Florence on 2 April 1566 and was given the name Catherine. Her family was well off and she got a good education from the Dominican sisters in S. Giovannino dei Cavalieri. Her parents, particularly her mother, were devout

---

1. F. Ribot, *The Book of the Institution of the First Monks*, Book 1, Chapter 2, trs B. Edwards, Oxford, Boars Hill, 1969, pp 3-4

Catholics and by the age of 10 she already had a rich spiritual life. She may have got her love for the eucharist from watching the way her mother received holy communion.[2] At the age of 10 she was able to express her desire to belong only to God by making a vow of chastity for life. When she was fourteen her father left home to take up an appointment as Commissioner in place called Cortona. Mary Magdalene was sent back as a boarder to S. Giovannino. The family priest, Pietro Blanca SJ insisted that she be allowed to receive holy communion on feastdays,[3] despite the fact that frequent communion was not the norm at that time. Later in her teens, when she was deciding what to do with her life, she knew that she wanted to be a nun and that she would join the Carmelite Monastery of Santa Maria degli Angeli in Florence because in the community the sisters were able to receive holy communion every day.[4]

She received the Carmelite habit on 30 January 1583 and entered the novitiate under the guidance of Sr Evangelista del Giocondo and the chaplain, Agostino Campi. After one year in the novitiate she would have been ready to make her first profession. However, the date of her profession had to be brought forward to 24 June 1584 as it was feared she would not live she was so ill at the time. Immediately following her profession she began to enjoy a period of forty days of ecstasy. These experiences were to continue, with some regularity, for the next twenty years of her life. Often she had requested of God the cessation of the embarrassing mystical gifts which set her apart from others. Yet she did not remain entirely free of them.[5] They would cease finally with her last illness, which began in 1604. This was the

---

2. See B. Secondin, *Santa Maria Maddalena de'Pazzi, Esperienza e dottrina*, Rome, Institutum Carmelitanum, 1974, p 99 and *Quaranta Giorni*, (The Forty Days), p 70

3. Later on another priest, Agostino Campi, the chaplain in the Carmelite monastery would have a significant influence on her love for the Mass. See Secondin, p 65 and *CO 1*, p 121

4. Breve Ragguaglio (Brief Summary) in *QG* pp 84-86. See also, Secondin, *op. cit.*, p 64. See note 7

5. J. Smet, *The Carmelites*, Vol. II, Darien, CSS, 1976, pp 217-219

beginning of a period of 'naked suffering' that would last until her death on 25 May 1607.

This form of ecstasy is described by her infirmarian who said that 'her face was most beautiful, her skin rosy … she did not seem to be the person illness had made thin and deathly pale'. In these moments which could be fleeting or could last many hours, her attention would be totally absorbed, she might remain still or she might move around the room or the chapel, in swift movements, sometimes miming what she was absorbed in, and through the expression on her face, the others would get an idea of what was going on for her. Her ecstasies, and what she said while in ecstasy, were recorded by the sisters in her community, charged by the chaplain, Agostino Campi, to do so.[6] Thus we have seven volumes of her works, which were published in Italian in their entirety only in the 1960s.[7]

The kind of experience she had

When endeavouring to examine the religious experience of St Mary Magdalene de'Pazzi we need to consider its context and

---

6. Early in the 1500s the church was built with pictures and statues of Carmelite saints. The community received it's first written constitutions between 1512 and 1513. Chaplains in the community in the late fifteenth century were Carmelites. Early in 1523 the care of the community was given to the diocesan clergy. Agostino Campi was chaplain between 1563 and 1591. The role of the chaplain included a certain governance and the care of the intellectual and spiritual life of the nuns as well as the normal liturgical duties. Campi brought Dominicans into the community. He provided a library. He had a good knowledge of the bible. He was the one who got the sisters to write down what Mary Magdalene said during her ecstasies. In the later years of her life Jesuits were introduced to the community.

7. I will refer to the works using abbreviations that come from their Italian titles: *I Quaranta Giorni* (The Forty Days) – *QG*; *I Colloqui*, 1 & 2 (The Dialogues 1 & 2) – *CO 1* and *CO 2*; *Renovatione della Chiesa* (The Renewal of the Church) – *RC*; *Revelatione et Intelligentie* (Revelation and Understanding) *RE*; *Probatione* 1 & 2 (Probation) *PR 1* and *PR 2*. A section of *QG* is called *Breve Ragguaglio* (Brief Summary) – *BR*, which is a short biography written by one of the sisters in her community. The translations are my own.

setting, its levels and content and the saint's own understanding of the experience.

Context and setting

We can distinguish three characteristic introductions to the descriptions of her ecstasies. Firstly, there were the occasions when she was called by God with the words: '*Vieni Sponsa mea*' (Come, my beloved) or words similar.[8] On these occasions her Lord and Spouse calls her in a personal way, to reveal his truth to her. Thus, for example, she is invited to enter the mystery of the Holy Spirit, at the beginning of the Eight Days of the Spirit,[9] or to see the work of the Word incarnate in the Trinity.[10] This type of invitation is found more towards the latter part of the *Colloqui* and in the *Revelatione e Intelligentie*. This, however, does not represent a steady progress in her coming to mystical union. This lack of any indication of progress distinguishes Mary Magdalene from many other mystics such as St Teresa of Avila and St John of the Cross who were able to trace the steps towards holiness in their lives. With Mary Magdalene there appear to be no steps: right from the beginning she was taken into the inner precincts of God's presence and there was no discernible pattern thereafter. Where we meet the language of the Spouses in her experiences we are reminded of the loving expression of the biblical Song of Songs, and of the *Spiritual Canticle* of St John of the Cross. In this sense Mary Magdalene's experience was mystical in the sense of someone who encounters God or truth or love and is transformed by the encounter.

There is a second type of beginning that we find in the book of the *Quaranta Giorni* (Forty Days) in which the most typical of the forms of introduction is: 'Just after receiving communion, I began to ponder ...'[11] The ecstasies took place in the meditation period after communion and are associated directly with the reception of communion. Where the saint refers back to the

8. *RE*, p 43
9. idem
10. *RE*, p 96
11. e.g. *QG*, p 101

gospel, as she often does, we should not forget an unusual practice in S. Maria degli Angeli in which communion was received,
not during the Mass but at a separate hour.[12] Despite the time
difference, however, the intimate association between the gospel
in the Mass, the receiving of communion and the reflection afterwards is obvious, giving a rhythm to the lives of the sisters that
was contemplative and liturgical.

On other occasions she begins simply by saying: 'as I pon-
dered the gospel of the day ...'[13] On these occasions she might
consider the actual text in detail[14] or be brought off to something
quite different, with very little direct relationship to the text.[15]
Nonetheless, the association of the experience with the gospel of
the day is unmistakeable.

Two other indications are worthy of mention: those in which
the verses of the Psalms read in the Office come to mind again
and again in the course of the day or in the course of a particular
ecstasy, giving further indication of a life steeped in the scriptures, and finally, those occasions when at any time of the day
she might be taken up in ecstasy: 'around midnight she went
into rapture' is the simple description given by the amanuensi
(notetakers). On these occasions there is no direct reference either to gospel or communion.

Experiences: levels and content
In the description of her encounters we are able to see that the
saint tasted and penetrated the truth of God and the truths of
Catholic faith. What we recite in the Creed, she held as the object
of her love, as something of which she was given an intimate
knowledge. There is a great chaos in much of the works of Mary
Magdalene and for this reason neat divisions and distinctions
are not easy to make. One way of approaching the matter is to
choose a number of texts that together will help to form a com-

12. B. Secondin, op. cit., p 65 97. *RE*, p 216
13. *QG* 109
14. *QG*, p 183
15. *RE*, p 216

plete treatment of the history of salvation centred in Christ, which we take to be the central line of thought that unites the oft chaotic thought and experience of the saint. While respecting the fact that in any one ecstasy there is a host of mystical graces present,[16] we will try to move along four lines:

a) the occasions when in a direct way she penetrates the mystery in its simplest form. These moments would seem to be the highest moments where words and images fail her and, after giving the briefest and simplest account of what she sees, she is reduced to silence;

b) the occasions in which she is given a detailed understanding of the scripture text in terms of analogy. These are on the second level because of the synthetic vision of the mystery contained in them, the ability of the contemplative to see things in their essential relationship, and in an instant, without the labour of discursive reasoning;

c) the most difficult level to treat is that on which, with a very rich symbolic language (taken from nature, the city, or the arts), she recounts her understanding of the theological mystery,[17] the situation of the church[18] or the situation in her own community.[19]

d) the last level is that on which the saint entered into and relived the events she was given to share with the Lord. The best example of this is the experience of one Holy Week in which she literally perspired and suffered with her Jesus.

---

16. C. Catena, *Introduzione a Colloqui*, p 21: 'We do not see just one, but a variety of mytical graces that are manifest all at the same time or that come one after the other without interruption, prolonging the ecstacy beyond anything that is humanly possible and filling it with events and images that are exceptional and unexpected. Rapture, flight of the spirit, revelations, formal discourses, mystical contemplation, and the addition of a striking external demeanour, that often accompanied the unusual phenomenon of her speaking.'

17. *RE*, pp 76-90, 150-170

18. *C0 1*, p 292, 371

19. *QG*, p 116-119; *Co 1*, pp 292f, 178, 360. See B. Secondin, *op. cit.*, pp 376-377

The content of her experiences:
a) Theological truths tasted and penetrated

– The Blessed Trinity
One of the striking things about the content of her experience is
the clarity she acquires in relation to the truths of our faith. Her
experiences give her an intimate grasp of the history of salvation
from before creation all the way through to the close of creation
and beyond. There are some very clear examples of this in the
volume of her works entitled *Revelatione et Intelligentie* (Revelations and Understanding). I have tried to capture her experience in the following poem, which is a collage of passages from
her writings that I put together some years ago:
>From all time and before
the Father looked at the Son
he looked deeply
and he loved what he saw
The Spirit was in the looking
and there was peace.
And the Son, the Word of God
looked at the Father
The Word looked deeply
and he loved what he saw
The Spirit was in the looking
and there was peace.
In the beginning of time
the Father and the Son
looked into themselves
They looked deeply
and they loved what they saw
and the Spirit was in the looking
and the whole of creation came into being
in God's own image and likeness
it came into being
and there was peace
God looked into creation and found Mary

God looked deeply
And loved what he saw
The Spirit was in the looking
and the Word became flesh
And the Word was peace
Mary looked at the Word
the issue of her womb
She looked deeply
and she loved what she saw
and the Spirit was in the looking
and there was peace.
And Jesus looked at the world
he looked deeply
and he loved what he saw
and he waits until the world looks back
and looks deeply
and loves what it sees
and the Spirit is in the looking
and there is peace.

Here I would like to emphasise the way in which she sat with the persons of the Trinity and saw them from the point of view of who they are (immanent) and what they do (economic). The use of the words *looking* and *looking deeply* are my words that attempt to translate those of the saint. They suggest something of the word *influire* that Mary Magdalene uses to express the persons of the Trinity flowing into one another. The concept of looking recalls the incidence of the people in the desert when they looked at the image of the serpent and were healed,[20] or the centurion who looks at the crucified Lord,[21] or Jesus looking at the rich young man.[22] It is a looking that has the power to influence both the one who looks and the one who is looked at.

---

20. Num 21:8: So Moses prayed for the people. 8 And the Lord said to Moses, 'Make a poisonous serpent, and set it on a pole; and everyone who is bitten shall look at it and live.'
21. Mk 15:19
22. Lk 18:24

Here is how the mystical text describes it:

... she flew once more, in the usual way, to the throne of the
Most Holy Trinity, to ponder the greatness of God and God's
immense goodness. There she saw the three Divine Persons,
speaking to one another, communicating their divine words
in ways that cannot be described. The Father was speaking to
the Son, and the Son was speaking to the Father in return.
The Father and the Son were speaking to the Spirit and the
Spirit was speaking to the Father and the Son in return and
they went on speaking all the time: the Father to the Son, the
Son returning the same words; the Father and the Son to the
Holy Spirit, the Holy Spirit back again to the Father and the
Father speaking again, now to the Son, now to the Holy Spirit
and they both speak again to the Father in a way that is impossible for us to understand; she, however, also saw all of
this in a way that pleased the Holy Trinity to show to her,
and in a way that lies within human capacity.'[23]

This passage is an example of the occasions in the early period
when the sisters engage the saint in conversation after the event.
For this reason the description lacks the intensity of later visions
recounted directly. The content is simple and the language is
that of the mystic without word; a continual succession of the
same words and the key word is one that to us, and to the
amanuensi (note-takers), could mean very little, namely *'influire'*
(speak, communicate, impress, influence, flow into). We are left
to speculate as to the exact meaning of this word in the mind of
the saint. If we were free to invent language we might say something like the persons of the Trinity word to one another: The
Father words to the Son and the Son words to the Father.

We pass on to her description of the activity of the Trinity
outside of itself, which is as follows:

That Most Holy Trinity then was speaking to every creature
that exists here on earth. And the Word, become flesh, was
speaking thus: by sending the gifts to all those creatures by

23. *C0 1*, pp 144-155

which they would be open to the actions of that Most Holy Trinity in such a way that the Holy Trinity would find pleasure in them. She saw then that the Father aspired for (*aspirare* – longed for) those creatures: 'I say (she said) that the Eternal Father aspired, that is, he desired the health of those creatures. It is said: this one aspired, longed for such a dignity, or such a thing, because he desires it, and seeks it with great longing.' It is something greater to long for than to desire: however, this blessed soul understood that the Eternal Father longed for our health, which means that he sought it with great longing, and there is nothing more than that that we can say. The Son respired, breathed in the creature, that is, he came to rest in the creature and made the creature pleasing to the Father, and to himself, and to the Holy Spirit. To respire means to rest, as we say sometimes, let me breath a little, which means, let me rest a little; let me rest a little and then I will do and say everything you want. The Holy Spirit inspired, which means that he continued to enlighten the creature, in order that the creature might grow in virtue and become increasingly pleasing and acceptable to God.'[24]

This is a continuation of the first passage cited and therefore another reflection after the event. We notice how the saint in this passage tries to explain what she saw in words that the sisters might understand. The doctrine is simple and clear, in as much as it could be clear; there is no intricate reasoning of imagery involved but just the simple statement of fact, within the limits of human language. We are given an understanding of the different roles of the Persons in the Trinity: the Father who takes the initiative in his desire for the salvation of his creatures, the Son who makes human persons pleasing to God by resting in them and the Spirit who enlightens human persons in all truths allowing them to grow in the favour of God.

24. *C0 1*, p 115

– The Incarnate Word

Once having established the primary role of the Father both within and outside the Trinity as the One who takes the initiative, our attention turns with Mary Magdalene to the mission and operation of the Son as the centre of all activity:

> When I had received communion, I reflected on those words of Saint John: 'In the beginning was the Word and the Word was with God and the Word was God'. It seemed to me that I understood that 'in the beginning' without any beginning, and without any end either. This beginning, and this end was the eternal Word generated by the Father. However, we say, the Word was, the Word was God himself, and the Word was with God. It seemed to me that this Word, that is, God, was with God, that is, was with himself. God was the Word, just like I said above, I said that the Word was God, so now I say that God is the Word, that God is the same, but there is a difference, since the Son is the Word because of being generated by the Father and the Son is God because of being one and the same with the Father.[25]

In some way we have to raise ourselves above the level of the mere words, simple in themselves but enriched by the sentiment of the one who pronounces them. It is not a matter of indifference to the saint that the Word is God. What she says is not mere repetition of a formula. We see in what she says a penetration of the truth which brings her joy and peace. In this light we begin ourselves to penetrate the language of the contemplative which of necessity is simple and, at first sight, even obvious, but is so laden with the attention of the heart that it is true understanding of which the human person alone, through the element of divinity in him, is capable. Moreover, in this case we have evidence, in the continuation of the passage cited, that what Mary Magdalene manages to convey in words is far from the whole truth:

> But it is one thing to look and see. It is something else to speak about what we have encountered. I know that there is

---

25. *QG*, p 154

> something here that I encountered, but I could not say nor
> could I find the words with which to explain it.[26]

The text she was contemplating was a liturgical text and the setting was the meditation after communion. We move on to consider in the words of the saint, how the Word who was God took
on human form in order that humankind might be given a share
in divinity:

> I could see then that the creature was nothing, and that God,
> and that the great God, in order to communicate this great-
> ness to the creature, hid his greatness from the creature so
> that the creature might become another God by participa-
> tion. 'O love, it was he in his infinite being, invisible, immor-
> tal, unequalled, who has the desire to become mortal, visible,
> and an equal, and that this should never end. He was rich,
> powerful, wise and full of all the treasures of the wisdom of
> God, and he desired to become poor and little, humble and
> initiated, so that the human race might become rich and
> mighty, wise and full of every virtue.[27]

The content of this passage is that God, in order to communicate
with creation, became part of creation. It is the doctrine of the
kenosis which we find in St Paul.[28] He who was rich became poor
so that humankind might be made rich.[29] In communicating
with men and women he made them divine by participation.
This idea of divinity by participation goes all through the works,
and emerges therefore as one of the characteristic doctrines of
Mary Magdalene. It may be paralleled to the idea of the union of
transformation in St John of the Cross.

Love is the only reason for God's wanting to communicate
with us and unite us to himself. In the next two passages the
theme of love is foremost: God created us out of love and
showed a still greater love in redeeming us. The greatest expression of that love is in the eucharist. After receiving communion

26. *QG*, p 155
27. *C0 1*, pp 93-94
28. Phil 2:5-9
29. 2 Cor 8:9-10

Mary Magdalene began her usual meditation and straight away, as she considered the Lord's saying 'I longed very much to eat this Passover with you', she was taken up in contemplation:

> I could see in the incarnation because of those two desires, the love that moved the Father to send the Word and the love that moved that same Word to come and take on our human-ity, as if the Father had said: Son of mine, I want you to take on human flesh. The Son replied: I desired it too. That does not mean that the Son desired it before the Father. It was only to show how ready he was to obey the Father. If, Father, this is your desire, that I should become human by taking on hu-manity, and that is what I wanted too, then I am more than happy to accept this Passover, this movement in which my Divinity can be united to humanity. It's not that God speaks or desires. It is a way of speaking that we can understand. Desire, therefore, means the love that moved the Father to give us his Word, the only-begotten Son; he wanted the love that moved the Son to come and the readiness of his obedi-ence. The love that moved the two Persons, the Father to send and the Son to come, is really the Holy Spirit who is the third Person of the Blessed Trinity, since in that movement to take on our humanity all three Persons were at work. That 'desire to eat this Passover with you' is the passage of Divinity to our humanity. As regards the union that God makes with the creature in this most holy sacrament, God is moved to make it by the same love that moved him to take on human form, I mean, to take on our humanity. There are two desires, i.e. I have a desire, and I desired, and the first is the love that moves the Divinity and the humanity of Jesus to-gether.[30]

This passage is another which suffers from the fact that it is re-counted after the event. We see in it the effort of the saint to ex-plain what she saw to her listeners. This passage might well have been put in the next section because there is an element of analogy in it with its play on the word *desiderio* (desire). I have

30. *C0 1*, p 223

included it here, seeing in it how Mary Magdalene was able to penetrate that total desire on Jesus' part to be with humankind, not merely by analogy but in essence. As in other passages, from the repetition of phrases, we saw a much more vivid experience than she was able to recapture after the event. It is a further example of her *visività*, her ability to see.[31]

Still on the same theme of love, we touch on one of the finer points of Christian doctrine, namely the greater love shown by God in the redemption in comparison to the creation. The point of discussion here, which has occupied the minds of Thomists and Scotists for centuries, is whether there would have been an incarnation had the first man not sinned. It is unlikely that her theological understanding came from one school or another. It seems to be purely her own, learned in the only school she knew, which was the Mass and the Divine Office.

The passage in question is the following:

'Here, listen and pay attention … My word brought to completion the love with which I want to glorify you, through that transformation which he underwent for you by spilling out his blood, which gave rise in me to a love towards you which brought to completion the love with which I want to glorify you before the Word should die and before the first man should commit sin. … I saw the completion in my Word, and the Word saw completion on the cross, of that love with which I wanted to give you glory, a glory that would be complete, and even before the Word should die I wanted to give that glory, yes, but in a way that would be very different. And if Adam had not sinned, I would have brought you into paradise, yes, and the Word would have become flesh, yes, but that would only have been in order to give glory and not to triumph. And the glory that I would have given you, in part already belonged to you since you would not have committed sin, since it is true that I created you with free will and choice. The glory that I would have given you would be so different to the glory I am giving you now, as the creature is

31. cf B. Secondin, *op. cit.*, p 205

different from me. ... How great indeed, my daughter, is the
glory I give you now!'[32]

We first note the literary character of this passage which is
different from those which we have just seen. In this latter section of *Dialogues* the saint speaks directly with God and for God,
and the sisters write down all she says during the actual ecstasy.
Thus the style is more poetic and intense and there are no
explanations on the part of the saint. The doctrine thus expressed in more immediate terms still possesses the same simplicity and charity. Added to this we have here an example of
the passages that we find in the latter part of the *Dialogues* and
later works in which we see how Mary Magdalene stops and re-
mains silent for long periods in between words. These are the
real contemplative moments. How long they lasted at a time we
do not know but we are led to believe that it is in these moments
that the mystic penetrated the mystery where words remained
as a burden and a distraction.

Another characteristic which we note is that here, as distinct
from the other passages we have already seen, we do not have
the words *intendere* (understand) and *vedere* (see) but rather a direct conversation with God, where the human faculties are as if
they did not exist.

The content centres on the perfection of God's love on the
cross illustrated by the final words of Jesus: *Consummatum est* (It
is finished).[33] The Father loved his creatures from the beginning
and prepared a glory for them that they would receive in the
Son; but there was still a greater glory that was to come through
the Son's expiring on the cross. In this the Son showed himself
both as the one who triumphs and the one who glorifies. The
love which God bore us in creation was to be superseded by this
greater love which was made possible in a paradoxical way by
the sin of Adam – *O felix culpa!* (O happy fault)

---

32. C0-2, p 227
33. Jn 19:30

– The Blood

Mary Magdalene had another point of encounter with the Second Person of the Blessed Trinity: she knew him as the Blood. All that was in the Son was in the Blood and all that was in the Word was in the Blood:

> It was communion time in the morning, and she was pondering the passion of Jesus crucified and the words that he said in the hospel came to her: In my Father's house there are many dwelling places. She saw before the eyes of her mind Jesus upon the cross; and she thought that the house of the eternal Father was the humanity of Jesus, crucified in that way. The dwelling places were all the wounds that Jesus had in his holy Body, but straight away she thought that the soul rests in those five which were the greatest and she saw that the Blood that came from each one of those wounds did something to the soul and made the soul do something also in return.
>
> (Then she speaks) I am saying that first, in the left foot, the blood brought it to nothing, and the soul came to know itself. In the right foot the blood purified it and the soul became strong. In the left hand the blood enlightened it and the soul grew in its knowledge of God. In the right hand the blood perfected it and the soul grew in charity. His side gave nourishment and the soul became transformed in the Blood, and could not think of anything other than Blood, taste anything other than Blood, feel anything other than Blood, think anything other than Blood or speak about anything other than Blood. Everything the soul would do would submerge it even more in that Blood such that the soul, now transformed in the Blood of Jesus, had become another him (Jesus), now able to say to other creatures those beautiful words of the prophet Isaiah: For my thoughts are not your thoughts, nor are your ways my ways, that the thoughts, the reflections and all the works of that soul so transformed in the blood of Jesus, are not like those of other creatures.[34]

---

34. *CO 1*, 96-98

This in an encounter with the Blood poured out and therefore with the death of Jesus in his great act of love. There is no explanation of the connection between this encounter with Blood and the blood of the eucharist, but it cannot be impossible to see: it was communion time in the morning and the saint was pondering the passion of Jesus Christ.

Before going to the section on analogy we wish to draw this first section to a close. It was the section in which we saw the highest level of Mary Magdalene's experience; those occasions when with clear and unhindered vision she saw, in the fullest sense possible, the mystery presented to her by God. This is the gift of the true contemplative, namely to see, without the process of reasoning, the objective reality placed before them in all its simplicity. Moreover, as we shall see, the verb 'see' is to be understood in its fullest sense as that total seeing in which there is both delight and understanding.

b) Theological truths: understood by analogy

The second kind of experience that Mary Magdalene enjoyed were those in which she was given an understanding of the liturgical texts, not in the form of simple statements but by an analogical penetration involving a unifying view of the truth contained in all the elements of the text. The vision on this level is somewhat more complicated than what we saw on the first level:

> Then when I had received communion I thought about the gospel of that Sunday: Now he was standing one day by the Lake of Gennesaret, with the crowd pressing round him listening to the word of God.[35] It seemed to me that the lake was the humanity of Jesus and Jesus who was standing on the shore of that lake was the Divinity and the crowd that was there was every man and woman, who, whether they know it or not, are in the lake that is the humanity of Jesus, made as they are in his image and likeness. It seems to me that the boat into which Jesus steps, Peter's boat, is the holy church, where Jesus now enters through the most holy sacrament. The other boat that Jesus does not get into, is the syna-

35. Lk 5:1

gogue of the Jews. The net that Peter uses to fish is the intellect and memory and Peter who casts the net is the will that did not want to cast out the net of intellect and memory. If he did not want the intellect to understand the things of God, and if the memory did not record the gifts of God, then the fish could never be caught, the fish who were the greatness of God and the knowledge of his gifts. The gospel then says that the apostles had fished all night and had caught nothing; thus the soul that fishes in the night of sin can never have knowledge of God or of his great favours. Peter then was washing the nets. He cleaned his nets because, since he had not caught anything, he found that they had picked up rubbish and twigs that were breaking them. It seemed to me that the soul, fishing in the night of sin, could find nothing other than rubbish and twigs to dirty and break the nets. Saying that Peter, whom we take to be the will, was washing and cleaning the nets, means that the soul that disposes itself through the sacrament of penance succeeds in this way in being freed from sin. Jesus then, standing by the lake, tells Peter to cast the net into the deep. When Peter does that he catches many fish. In the same way, the soul, washed in the waters of confession and cleansed by penance, hears Jesus telling it through internal inspirations to cast out into the deep like Peter, thus showing how Jesus says to the will to get the intellect and the memory to be attentive to God and to remember God. When the soul obeys this command, it catches those great big fish of the knowledge of God and of his gifts … When the soul succeeds in having knowledge of God and of itself, it comes to unity with God and does the things of God. Then I saw that the water of this lake was still and did not move like the water of the rivers. Here I saw the immutability of God as God says of himself, I am God and I do not change. (*Ego sum Deus, e non mutor*).[36] This God is always of the one will and the one desire.[37]

---

36. Mal 3:6
37. *QG*, pp 183-185

The vision begins with the words, *mi pareva*, (it seemed to me) which suggests that here we are dealing with one of less intensity and directness than those that begin with *vedevo* (I could see).

By her use of *mi pareva*, therefore, she begins to draw the analogy between the gospel description and history of salvation. The person of Jesus represents the divinity and is therefore the principle agent in the event. The place where the event takes place, the only place where such an event could take place, was in the water of the lake, which she sees as the humanity of Christ, thus indicating the necessity of his mediation. Christ's activity takes effect in the church – Peter's boat – in which those inside, through an act of the will which moves the intellect and memory – casting the nets – receive knowledge of the things of God which, when they overflow the boat which is the church, are taken up and received by the other boat into which Jesus did not enter at first.

In order to be able to receive the wonders of God the nets must be strong and clean of all that might tear them. This strengthening and cleansing is the work carried out in the sacrament of penance and the fisherman no longer go fishing in the night of sin but in the light of Christ which is free from sin.

The content and the association of images is very clear and not one element of the account in the gospel was left un-interpreted. This takes us beyond the level of simple meditation where the mind tries to wrestle with the many aspects of the subject at hand. The tone of the passage we have cited suggests a striking unity between the elements involved. There is no indication of how long the contemplation lasted other than the fact that these periods of prayer after communion usually lasted two hours. One does not get the impression that in that two-hour period she struggled with the various elements until she finally managed to tie them together. Rather, there is the impression of an instantaneous unifying view in which the essential connections were seen in their entirety without the labour of discursive reasoning. In this we understand the capacity of the contemplation to see the essential truth of things in a way that is sheer gift.

This is one of the relatively rare occasions in which Mary Magdalene uses the standard psychological terminology of intellect, memory and will. Unlike the Spanish masters, Teresa and John of the Cross, she seldom stopped to examine the psychological process by which the soul was united with its spouse. Her view of the relationship was more taken for granted as something lived, without detailed reflection, a love affair that the lovers would never think of analysing.

The following passage brings out this aspect of the warmth of the relationship between Mary Magdalene and her lover.[38] It is based on the gospel of the Good Shepherd, which was the gospel of the Mass of that day.

This loving Word, the chief shepherd and loving shepherd, goes into the gentle and joyful sheepfold of his church, given to me as the gate and the sheepfold, where he gives his sheep the clean water of his grace ... grace which is really the gate through which the Word enters the soul, but he doesn't enter in the form of any creature or anything less than himself, but only with his own grace giving himself to that soul. He would never go in through the window because he would never want to enter the soul unless the soul had given consent; which means that our will is always the gate by which the good shepherd can enter. ... And as the true shepherd of that church he takes up the staff of his own love and he takes up fear as well, and he calls with his gentle and pleasing voice and all those who belong to his flock hear his voice that says: Return to me with your whole heart.[39] ... Calling all the believers to repentance and promising them the kingdom of heaven. He is not like the thief that comes in to steal. He comes to give his own grace, filling the soul with his gifts – urging it and calling it with great love, showing the soul his own delight and letting the soul taste it again.[40]

---

38. See also the dialogue in *Colloqui* beginning with the 46th dialogue, *CO 2*, 195f
39. Joel 2:12
40. *RE*, pp 133-134

The passage is taken from the forth volume of her works, *Revelatione e Intelligentie* and thus the words are those that are taken down directly by the other sisters. All the depth of feeling of the saint is captured along with the moments of contemplative silence indicated by the dots. The expressions are affectionate – spoken by one whose love and admiration are perceptible. What adds warmth to the description is the use of the adjectives pleasing, joyful, gentle. It reminds us of the notion of 'loving attention' in the doctrine of St John of the Cross.[41]

Mary Magdalene and the Eucharist
We began with Mary Magdalene's earliest experiences of the eucharist and spoke about how her love for the eucharist led her to be a Carmelite nun. In her experiences of faith she received a knowledge of being loved by God in the *humanified*[42] Christ. She received this love intimately through the power of the word that was read in the eucharist and the other moments of liturgical prayer in the life of the community. And she received it in the reception of holy communion, in which she understood that she was receiving the blood of Christ that meant for her Christ himself, her beloved. Out of this experience she fulfilled the ideals of the Carmelite life and became for her community the loving sister that served to build up the community in grace.

The blessed sacrament became for her the way to union with God in the power and love of the Word. It gave her knowledge of salvation and allowed her to capture in her love and understanding the extent of the history of salvation and to see the role of the church in the working out of that history. Her experience of the written word was an experience of communication with Divinity in humanity, all that the word read at Mass is intended to be. This was made possible through the formation and rhythm of the life of a contemplative community. Her experi-

41. St John of the Cross, *Ascent of Mount Carmel*, II, 12, 8
42. The word in Italian is *umanato* which could be translated as, made flesh, become human, incarnate, but these might not capture the full sense of the Word becoming human as being made human through the will of the Father and the work of the Holy Spirit.

ence however did not stay in step with that rhythm or that formation. It went beyond that both in time and intensity.

For us today, we might see our celebration of the eucharist
more and more as an encounter with God in the Incarnate Word
and see more clearly the relationship that exists between the
Word and holy communion. In the words of Adrian Nocent: 'Is
it possible perhaps that there is a Carmelite way to celebrate the
liturgy of the Word and prayer? ..... Is it not something very
Carmelite to receive the Word of God, as a living and vibrant
word, and transmit it to others in all his strength? Is that not the
Carmelite ideal? And is that not the essence of being
prophetic?'[43]

Bibliography

1. de'Pazzi, Maria Maddalena, *Tutte le Opere*, 7 vols, eds. Bruno
   Nardini, Bruno Visentin, Carlo Catena, Giulio Agresti,
   Florence, Nardini, 1960-1966

2. de'Pazzi, Maria Maddalena, *The Complete Works of Saint Mary
   Magdalen de'Pazzi*, trs G. Pausback, O Carm, Fatima, Carmelite
   Fathers, 1969

3. Larkin, Ernest, O Carm, 'The Ecstasies of the Forty Days of
   Saint Mary Magdalene de'Pazzi,' *Carmelus* I (1954) 29-71

4. Maria Maddalena de'Pazzi, *Selected Revelations*, The Classics
   of Western Spirituality, trs and intro, Armando Maggi, New
   Jersey, Paulist Press, 2000

5. Nocent, Adrian, OSB, 'Actualisation et personalisation de la
   prière liturgique', *Carmelus*, 22 (1975) pp 119-135

6. Secondin, Bruno, O Carm, *Santa Maria Maddalena de'Pazzi,
   Esperienza e dottrina*, Rome, Institutum Carmelitanum, 1974

7. Smet, Joachim, O Carm, *The Carmelites*, Vol II, Darien, CSS,
   1976

---

43. A. Nocent OSB, 'Actualisation et personalisation de la prière
liturgique', *Carmelus*, 22 (1975) p 124

CHAPTER SIX

The Eucharist in the Carmelite Rule

Pat Mullins O Carm

On 1 October 1247, Pope Innocent IV issued his *Quae honorem Conditoris* commanding Carmelites to accept the 'proclaimed, corrected, and mitigated' rule he had drawn up for them. Pope Innocent's Rule (*regula bullata*) was a modified form of the 'formula of life (*vitae formula*)' written in accordance with the 'proposal (*propositum*)' of the Latin hermits on Mount Carmel by Patriarch Albert of Jerusalem about 40 years previously. Born about 1150 in Italy, Albert became one of the first canons regular of [the Holy Cross of] Mortara, Pavia, when that congregation was founded in 1180, before becoming bishop of Bobbio in 1184 and, less than a year later, in 1185, bishop of Vercelli. After twenty years as bishop of Vercelli, he was named Patriarch of Jerusalem in 1205. Because Saladin, the leader of the Saracens, had recaptured Jerusalem from the crusader armies in 1187, Albert's predecessor had chosen to live at Acre (after the crusaders had retaken that city in 1191). Sometime during the patriarchate of Albert (1206-1214), a group of Latin hermits on Mount Carmel, about 25 kilometres from Acre, who had formed a group under the leadership of a man known only as 'B,' asked Albert to write down a 'formula of life (*vitae formula*),' in keeping with the way of life they had chosen. His *Formula of Life* is a short text of only a few pages and it has traditionally been divided into twenty four short sections known as chapters.

Chapter 14 of the Carmelite Rule promulgated by Pope Innocent IV in 1247 follows the text written by Patriarch Albert of Jerusalem between 1206 and 1214 with only minor variations.

Albert's Formula of Life (Latin):	Albert's Formula of Life (Translation):
Oratorium, prout comodius fieri poterit, construatur in medio cellularum, ubi 'mane per singulas dies' (Lev 6:12, Vulgate) ad audienda missarum sollemnia convenire debeatis, ubi commode fieri poterit.	According as it will have been possible to be done more conveniently, an oratory is to be built in the middle of the cells where, when it will have been possible to be done conveniently, you ought to gather 'in the morning each day' (Lev 6:12, Vulgate) for hearing the solemnities of the Mass.

Building an Oratory for Hearing Mass

Apart from their regular encounters with whoever distributed their food and other basic necessities to them in their cells (see chapter 12), and the weekly meeting for fraternal correction (see chapter 15), it was only during 'the solemnities of the Mass' every morning that the hermit brothers encountered one another. The hermit-brothers were to recite the psalms privately, in their own cells (see chapter 11) and the primary purpose of the oratory was to provide a place where the hermit-brothers could gather to hear Mass.[1] It was also, presumably, the place where the weekly meetings for fraternal correction took place.

Albert's use of the term 'oratory (*oratorium*)' rather than 'church (*ecclesia*)' is probably significant from a juridical point of view. Although the situation would change as the Mendicants in Europe established their oratories as public chapels, at the time when Albert wrote the *Formula of Life*, an oratory, unlike a church, was not permitted to use a bell (to call the public to Mass) and a public Mass could only be celebrated in an oratory by permission of the local ordinary.[2] The oratory, in other

---

1. See Rudolf Hendriks, O Carm, 'The Original Inspiration of the Carmelite Order as Expressed in the Rule of Saint Albert,' in *The Rule of Saint Albert*, trs Brocard Sewell O Carm, *Vinea Carmeli 1*, Aylesford - Kensington, 1973, pp 65-72 at 70

2. See S. Teuws, O Carm, 'De evolutione privilegiorum Ordinis Carmelitarum usque ad Concilium Tridentinum,' *Carmelus* 6 (1959) 173-175; Bede Edwards ODC, 'The Rule of Saint Albert: The Latin Text Edited with an English Translation,' in *The Rule of Saint Albert*, *Vinea Carmeli* 1, Aylesford - Kensington, Carmelite Book Service, 1973, pp 73-93 at 85 n 23; Theodulf Vrakking with Joachin Smet, O Carm, 'Albert's

words, was intended exclusively for the use of the hermit-brothers themselves and no public Mass was envisaged.

In 1228, the Pope imposed the ecclesiastical penalty of interdict on the Patriarchate of Jerusalem after the German Emperor, Frederick II, who had been excommunicated for failing to lead the promised sixth crusade, crowned himself King of Jerusalem. This interdict prevented the hermit brothers on Mount Carmel, which was part of the Patriarchate of Jerusalem, from having Mass every day as their formula of life prescribed. In the following twelve months, the economic and other effects of the interdict seem to have undermined some of the hermit brothers and, just over a year later, in April 1229, the Prior requested powers from the Pope to absolve those who, seeking economic security, had left the hermitage to be ordained, or to exercise the ordained ministry elsewhere. The Prior may also have asked the Pope to exempt the Carmelites from the interdict for, on 9 April 1229, Pope Gregory IX's *Religionis vestrae* took the hermit brothers of Mount Carmel under the protection of the Holy See and allowed them to celebrate Mass behind closed doors in time of interdict. The fact that their chapel was technically an 'oratory (*oratorium*)' intended for the exclusive use of the hermit brothers probably facilitated this decision which enabled them to resume the practice of hearing the solemnities of the Mass in the morning each day.

Gathering in the Morning Each Day to Hear Mass
In view of the fact that, already by the late twelfth century,[3] and certainly by the late thirteenth century,[4] '*audire missam*' had the

Formula for Living,' in *Carmelite Rule: Introduction, Translation into Dutch and Annotations*, Almelo, Netherlands, Dutch Carmelite Province, 1979, pp 11-49 at 30 n 46

3. See R. E. Latham, *Revised Medieval Latin Word-List from British and Irish Sources*, trs, ed, London, Oxford University Press, 1965, p 37

4. See Roy J. Deferrari, Sr M Inviolata Barry CDP, and Ignatius McGuiness OP, *A Lexicon of St Thomas Aquinas based on the Summa Theologica and Selected Passages of his Other Works*, Baltimore Md, Catholic University of America Press, 1948, p 985.

meaning of 'to assist at, or take part in, Mass,' it is possible that Albert may have understood '*ad audienda missarum sollemnia*' as meaning 'to assist at, or take part in, the solemnities of the Mass'. It is probably from this perspective that, during the 1970s, the commentary by the Dutch scholars, Vrakking and Smet, translated *ad audienda* as 'to celebrate.'[5] The translation 'to hear,' used by both Edwards[6] and Chandler,[7] should probably be preferred, however, because the surviving documents of the Canons of Mortara,[8] to which Albert belonged, and the other surviving documents of which Albert was author, or co-author,[9] all use the verb *audire* in the sense of 'to hear' or 'to listen to.' The letter of approval and *propositum vitae* of the Third Order of the Humiati, to which Albert contributed in 1201, includes the phrase: 'You are to gather in a suitable place each Sunday for hearing the word of God (*singulis diebus dominicis ad audiendum Dei verbum in loco idoneo convenire*).'[10] The similarity between this phrase and the prescription in Albert's *Formula of Life*, and the strong emphasis on meditating on the law of the Lord (see chapter 10) and on the Word of God as the sword of the spirit (see chapter 19), suggests that, as well as 'hearing' the Mass as such, Albert's use of '*ad audienda*' may also have carried the connotation of listening to or hearing the Word of God at Mass.

In the Apostolic and post-Apostolic age, there do not seem to have been any fixed precepts regarding the hour at which the

---

5. See Vrakking O Carm, 'Albert's Formula for Living' at 31.
6. See Edwards ODC, 'Translation' at 85.
7. See Paul Chandler O Carm, *The Rule of Saint Albert*, Victoria, Carmelite Library, 2003, p 39
8. See Vincenzo Mosca O Carm, *Alberto Patriarca di Gerusalemme: Tempo -Vita - Opera*, Rome, Edizioni Carmelitane, 1996, pp 563 line 46, 565/126, 571/373, 578/620 and 627-628, 579/658 and 659, 581/734, 582/755, 583/779, 588/964, 589/1004, 592/1105-1107 and 1124, 595/1209, 597/1293, 602/118, 607/375 and 380, 611/550 and 553, 615/773, 616/796 and 805 and 818.
9. See ibid, pp 630/20, 634/24 and 25, 636/22, 642/48, 643/ 64, 646/36-37, 666/31 and 37, 667/41, 670/159, 672/231 and 239, 673/265, 674/291, 676/372-373, 677/386 and 391, 679/467, 684/631.
10. See ibid, p 689/148-149

eucharistic celebration should take place. The Last Supper was
held in the evening and it seems that the apostle Paul 'broke
bread' about midnight (see Acts 20:7). About the year 114 AD,
however, Pliny the Younger, who was governor of Bithynia, was
probably referring to the eucharist when he reported that
Christians assembled in the early hours of the morning and
bound themselves by a *sacramentum* (oath). Tertullian suggests
that Christians assembled for the eucharist (well) 'before dawn
(*antelucanis aetibus*).'[11] From sometime in the third century, the
celebration of Mass was delayed until shortly before dawn and
this change seems to have been motivated by a recognition that
the Saviour's resurrection occurred in the morning before sun-
rise. Cyprian, for example, comments about the Sunday celebration: 'We celebrate the resurrection of the Lord in the morning.'[12]
During the fourth century, the clergy from the local village came
to celebrate Mass for the monks of the monastery of St
Pachomius in Egypt on Sunday mornings. The time of celebration may have been motivated by the time of the resurrection or,
perhaps, by considerations relating to the monastic timetable.[13]
From about the fifth century, the 'third hour' (0900 hrs) came to
be regarded as 'canonical' for the solemn Mass on Sundays and
feastdays.

Noting that the verb *convenire* 'is a technical term used to sig-
nify assembling for "community exercises",' Vrakking/Smet
point out that, in the actual circumstances of the hermits on
Mount Carmel, 'it meant quite literally that one left one's separate lodgings to go to the oratory, located as centrally as possible.'[14] The instruction that the hermit-brothers ought to gather
for hearing the solemnities of the Mass suggests that Albert had
in mind the equivalent of a conventual or capitular Mass (*Missa
conventualis* or *capitularis*). During the early medieval period, a

---

11. Tertullian, *De cor. mil.*, 3
12, Cyprian, *Ep.*, 63
13. See A. Veielleux, *La liturgie dans le cénobitisme pachômien au IVe siècle*,
StudAns 57, Rome, 1968, pp 230-241
14. See Vrakking O Carm, 'Albert's Formula for Living' at 31 n 49

daily conventual Mass was normative in monastic communities and in the communities of canons regular. Various different terms are used to describe such conventual Masses during the early to high middle ages: Canonical Mass (*Missa canonica*), Capitular Mass (*Missa capitularis*), Principal Mass (*Missa prae-cipua*), Major Mass (*Missa maior*), Mass of Terce (*Missa Tertiae*), Mass celebrated conventually (*Missa conventualiter celebrata*), Mass in the convent (*Missa in conventu*).[15] In the communities of monks and canons, the conventual Mass was always a high or solemn Mass (*Missa solemnis*),[16] though it was less solemn on fe-rias than on Sundays or any other feast. It allowed only a single priest celebrant[17] and was normally sung or chanted with the as-sistance of a choir at the high altar[18] 'after the hour of Terce on ordinary days; after Sext on simple and ferial days; after None on fast days.'[19] As a member of the Canons of Mortara, Albert was himself familiar with a situation in which various Masses were celebrated each day, one of which, described as the 'Major Mass (*Missa maior*)' was designated as the conventual Mass.

The formal prescription of daily Mass in Albert's *Formula of Life* was somewhat unusual. Rudolf Hendriks comments that no other rule for hermits included such an explicit emphasis on daily Mass[20] and Vrakking/Smet say that the 'obligation of "cel-ebrating the eucharist daily" appears to be unique in the first

15. See A. Sanna and J. Grigomont, 'Messa conventuale' in *Dizionario degli Instituti di Perfezione,* ed Guerrino Pellicia and Giancarlo Rocca, 14 vols, Rome, Edizioni Pauline, 1974-2005, 4:1249-1259 at 1250-1252
16. Adrian Fortesque, *The Mass. A Study of the Roman Liturgy,* London, Longmans, Green and Co, 1937, p 191
17. See A. Sanna and J. Grigomont, 'Messa conventuale' in *Dizionario degli Instituti di Perfezione,* ed. Pellicia and Rocca, 4:1249-1259 at 1253
18. See S. J. P. Van Dijk OFM and J. Hazalden Walker, *The Origins of the Modern Roman Liturgy. The Liturgy of the Papal Court and the Franciscan Order in the Thirteenth Century,* London, Darton, Longman and Todd, 1960, p 293
19. Jean Leclercq, 'Messe,' in *Dictionnaire d'archéologie chrétienne et de liturgie* vol 11/1, Paris, Letouzey et Ané, 1907-1950, pp 514-774 at 772 See Fortesque, *The Mass. A Study of the Roman Liturgy* pp 191-192.
20. See Hendriks O Carm, 'Inspiration' at 70

half of the thirteenth century.'[21] Bede Edwards describes it as 'highly original'[22] and the Carmelite liturgist, James Boyce, describes it as 'unusual.'[23] In his recent study on Albert of Jerusalem, Vincenzo Mosca O Carm describes daily Mass as 'a particular feature, possibly the only original observance'[24] in Albert's *Formula of Life*. It was not without precedent, however. Daily eucharist was regarded as part of the vocation of those members of monastic communities who followed a solitary lifestyle. The Regola Solitariorum,[25] written by the priest Grimlaic(us)[26] at the end of the ninth or in the early tenth century, was not intended for hermits or anchorites as such, but for those monks (*inclusos*) who had received approval to live a solitary lifestyle in close association with their particular monastery.[27] Regarded as the most ancient of the rules for such solitaries,[28] it points out that that the 'holy Fathers' (Apollonius, who was one of the Desert Fathers,[29] Augustine,[30] and Pope St Gregory the

21. See Vrakking, O Carm, 'Albert's Formula for Living' at 24 n 31

22. See Edwards ODC, 'Translation' at 85 n 25

23. See James Boyce, O Carm, *Carmelite Liturgical Spirituality*, Carmelite Spiritual Directory Project, Horizons 12, Melbourne, Carmelite Communications, 2000, p 14

24. 'una nota particolare, forse la sola osservanza originale,' see Mosca O Carm, *Alberto*, p 491

25. See PL 103:575-664

26. Little is known about Grimlaic apart from his being a priest and a recluse. See Armin Basedow, *Die Inclusen in Deutschland*, Heidelburg, J. Horning, 1895, p 10

27. See *Regola Solitariorum* (PL 103:574-575)

28. See Émile Bertaud, 'Dévotion eucharistique' in *Dictionnaire de Spiritualité*, Paris, Beauchesne, 1937-1995, 4:1621-1637 at 1623

29. The *Regola Solitariorum* (PL 103:625) quotes Apollonius, one of the Desert Fathers from the Thebaid, as saying that monks 'should as far as possible receive the mysteries of Christ daily (*ut, si fieri posset, quotidie communicarent mysteriis Christi*)' for 'the one who receives this more frequently without doubt receives the Saviour himself (*Qui autem, inquit, frequentius hoc suscipit, frequentius ipsum sine dubio Salvatorem suscipit*).' *Vitae Patrum* 2:7 (PL 21:418-419).

30. The *Regola Solitariorum* (PL 103:626) quotes St Augustine as saying: 'Thus nothing should make a Christian more afraid than to separate him/herself from the body of Christ. For if one is separated from the body of Christ, one is not a member of him; and if one is not a member

Great[31] are mentioned specifically) recommended that solitaries celebrate Mass or receive the body and blood of Christ every day.[32] Generally speaking, those hermits who did not belong to a monastic community would not have attended a communal daily Mass but, towards the end of the twelfth century, this began to change and the congregation of Austin Hermits, founded by Pope Gregory VIII in 1186, celebrated one Mass each day in their communities.[33]

Boyce comments that the fact that the *Formula of Life* 'prescribes that Mass be celebrated communally each day' shows that 'great importance was attached to the eucharistic celebration.'[34] The prescription was not absolute, however, and Albert recognised that it might not always be possible. Vrakking/Smet suggest that the circumstances that would make gathering for Mass impossible were 'if there was no priest' or in a situation 'where some separate living quarters were so far from the oratory that bad weather or personal reasons made it difficult to at-

---

of him, one's spirit will not be nourished. As the Apostle says: "Whoever does not have the spirit of Christ is not his [Rom 8:9] (*Nihil sic debet formidare Christianus quam separari a corpore Christi. Si enim separatur a corpore Christi, non est membrum ejus; si non est membrum ejus, not vegetatur spiritus ejus. Unde ait Apostolus: Quisquis spiritum Christi non habet, nic non est ejus* [Rom viii, 9])." See Augustine, *Tractatus in Ioannis Evangelium* 27.6 (PL 35:1618)

31. The *Regola Solitariorum* (PL 103:625) quotes Pope St Gregory the Great's *Dialogues* as saying that 'we ought ... to immolate the sacrifice of his body and blood daily (*Debemus ... quotidianas carnis et sanguinis ejus hostias immolare*).' See Gregory the Great, *Dialogi de vita et miraculis patrum Italicorum* 4:58 (PL 77:425). It also refers to the same text as praising Bishop Cassius of Narni (d. 558) 'who used to offer the sacrifice to God daily (*qui quotidianum sacrificium Deo offere consueverat*).' See Gregory the Great, *Dialogi de vita et miraculis patrum Italicorum* 4:56 (PL 77:421)

32. '*Non mea itaque opinione, sed sanctorum Patrum assertione haec utraque reor fieri posse, id est, et missas quotidie celebrare, et sacrosancta corporis et sanguinis Domini mysteria quotidie cum tremore et eimore sumere ...* ' See *Regola Solitariorum* 36 (PL 103:625)

33. See Pope Gregory VIII, *Epistola 1* (PL 136:645). See Van Dijk OFM and Hazalden Walker, *The Origins of the Modern Roman Liturgy*, p 51

34. See Boyce O.Carm, Carmelite Liturgical Spirituality p. 14

tend.'[35] The phrase 'when it will have been possible to be done
conveniently' is one of Albert's discretionary phrases, and another example of the governing principle with which the
Formula of Life ends: 'Discretion, however, which is the moderator
of the virtues, is to be used.'

Edwards suggests that Albert's prescription of daily Mass
may be based on the Constitutions of Albert's own order, the
Canons Regular of Mortara, or on the Statutes of the Canons of
Buiella or the Rule of the Humiliati, which he had composed.[36]
Neither of these documents specifically prescribes daily Mass
but the six references to the 'major Mass (*maior Missa*)'[37] in the
surviving section (October to April) of the Liturgical Customs of
the Canons Regular of Mortara show that Albert belonged to a
group where a conventual daily Mass was the norm.[38] The
canonist, Carlo Cicconetti O Carm, who produced a major study
of the rule in 1973, points out that, by the thirteenth century, the
majority of religious communities were coming together for the
eucharist every day[39] and Albert may have regarded daily Mass
as normative for those following the cenobitic lifestyle. Initially
(chapters 1-3) describing them as 'hermits (*eremitis*),' Albert

35. See Vrakking O Carm, 'Albert's Formula for Living' at 31 n 49
36. See Bede Edwards ODC, 'An Introduction to the Rule of Saint
Albert,' in *The Rule of Saint Albert*, trs *Vinea Carmeli 1*, Aylesford -
Kensington, Carmelite Book Service, 1973, pp 9-41 at 14
37. See appendix 2, 'Le Consuetudini Mortariensi' in Mosca O Carm,
Alberto, pp 599-617 at 600/61, 605/276-277, 611/566-567, 612/620,
616/799, 617/847
38. The term 'major Mass (*maior Missa*)' suggests that, like the monks at
Cluny, the Canons Regular of Mortara may also have had a second
daily conventual Mass, sometimes known as the *Missa matutinalis*, in
addition to the major conventual Mass, the *maior Missa*. See Joseph A.
Jungmann SJ, *Missarum Sollemnia. Eine genetische Erklärung der römis-
chen Messe*, Vienna, Herder, 1948, 1:259 = Joseph A. Jungmann SJ, *The
Mass of the Roman Rite. Its Origins and Development (Missarum Sollemnia)*,
trs Francis A. Brunner CSSR, Charles K. Riepe ed, London, Burns and
Oates, 1959, pp 151-152
39. See Carlo Cicconetti O Carm, *The Rule of Carmel, An Abridgement of the
translation by Gabriel Pausback O Carm*, ed Paul Hoban O Carm, trs Gabriel
Pausback, Darien, Illinois, Carmelite Spiritual Centre, 1984, p 274.

later, and more frequently (chapters 4, 5, 6, 8, 12, 13 and 15), refers to the group as 'brothers (*fratres*)' and it seems likely that the *propositum* that B and the other hermits on Mount Carmel submitted to Albert (see chapter 3) envisaged a lifestyle as hermits-in-community. If so, the prescription of a common oratory and of daily Mass may have been intended by Albert as one of the ways of introducing a communal/fraternal dimension into their essentially individual/solitary way of life.[40] Hendriks suggests that the primary purpose of daily Mass was 'so that daily they might encounter Christ in the sacred mysteries.'[41] Perhaps Albert deliberately arranged that, by encountering one another only in the oratory, either for Mass (chapter 14) or for fraternal correction (chapter 15), their mutual relationships would always take place in the context of an encounter with Christ.

Edwards,[42] Hendriks,[43] and *La Regola del Carmelo oggi*[44] regard the phrase 'in the morning each day (*mane per singulos dies*)' as a quotation from the Vulgate text of Lev 6:12,[45] where the Old Testament priest is described as ensuring that the fire on the altar never goes out by adding wood 'in the morning, each day (*mane per singulos dies*)' in preparation for the morning and evening holocausts. The holocausts included the cereal offerings, which were burned as a whole offering twice a day, and the sin offering of the High Priest (all of which was consumed by the fire). The meat of the other animals offered as sin, guilt of

40. See Otger Steggink O Carm, 'Fraternità e possesso in commune: l'ispirazione presso i mendicanti,' *Carmelus* 15 (1968) 10-20; Joseph Boudry OCD, 'Solitude et fraternité aux origines du Carmel,' *Carmel* 5 (1971) 84-106; Edwards ODC, 'Introduction' at 18

41. See Hendriks O Carm, 'Inspiration' at 70

42. See Bede Edwards ODC, 'The Rule of Saint Albert: The Latin Text Edited with an English Translation,' ibid, Carmelite Book Service, pp 73-93 at 84-85 n 24

43. See Rudolf Hendriks O Carm, 'The Original Inspiration of the Carmelite Order as Expressed in the Rule of Saint Albert,' ibid, trs Brocard Sewell O Carm, pp 65-72 at 70 n 17

44. See *La Regola del Carmelo oggi. Atti del Congresso Carmelitano, Roma/Sassone, 11-14 ottobre 1982*, ed Bruno Secondin O Carm, Rome, Institutum Carmelitanum, 1982, pp 11-25

45. This verse is listed as Lev 6:5 in some bibles

'peace/communion' offerings, was eaten by the priests but the internal organs connected with the more vital life processes, and any fat attached to those organs, were burned as part of the daily holocaust.[46] According to Faley, 'The perpetual fire, a characteristic of Persian cult, served as an uninterrupted prayer of the Hebrew community to the Lord.'[47] If Albert did indeed have the Vulgate text of Leviticus 6:12 in mind, he may have been making a deliberate association between the eucharist and the burnt sacrifices of the Old Testament and, in particular, between perpetual prayer and the perpetual fire on the altar of holocaust while, at the same time, prescribing the time of day and the frequency[48] of the celebration of the solemnities of the Mass.

Albert's Use of the Term 'Solemnities of the Mass'
The hermit-brothers were to gather for hearing the solemnities of the Mass (*ad audienda missarum sollemnia*). Some translators read '*missarum sollemnia*' simply as 'Mass,'[49] which might be appropriate if Albert's text had read '*ad audiendam missam.*' Boyce does not seem to regard the expression *missarum sollemnia* as significant either when he comments that, although the *Formula of Life* 'prescribes that Mass be celebrated communally each day,

46. Roland J. Faley TOR, 'Leviticus,' in *The New Jerome Biblical Commentary*, London, Geoffrey Chapman, 1993, pp 61-79 at 65
47. Ibid, at 65
48. The other texts cited in this context by *La Regola del Carmelo oggi*, ed. Secondin O Carm, are: Ps 145 (144):2 'Every day I shall bless you (*in omni die benedicam tibi*)'; Acts 2:46 'Each day ... breaking bread near their homes they ate their food with gladness and simplicity of heart (*cotidie ... frangentes circa domos panem sumebant cibum cum exultatione et simplicitate cordis*)'; Ezek 46:13-15 'Every day he must offer an unblemished lamb one year old as a burnt offering to Yahweh; he must offer this every morning (*et agnum eiusdem anni inmaculatum faciet holocaustum cotidie Domino semper mane faciet illud*).' Acts 2:46 is also cited in this context by Boudry OCD, 'Solitude et fraternité aux origines du Carmel' at 104
49. See Edwards ODC, 'Translation' at 85; Christopher O'Donnell O Carm, 'The Rule of Albert as Approved by Innocent IV (1247). A Revised Translation of the Carmelite Rule,' in *Ascending the Mountain: The Carmelite Rule Today*, Dublin, Columba Press, 2004, at 135; Chandler O Carm, *The Rule of Saint Albert*, p 39

virtually nothing specific is indicated as to how it should be rendered'.[50] However, since the texts associated with Albert's own order, and those of which he himself was author or co-author, appear to make a distinction between 'Mass (*missa*)' as such and the 'solemnities of the Mass (*missarum sollemnia*)' in particular, it is important to explore what exactly Albert may have understood by the term 'solemnities of the Mass (*missarum sollemnia*).'

The plural noun *sollemnia* can refer to sacred festivals or observances[51] and both Tertullian[52] and Cyprian[53] use it to describe the eucharist. When later writers use *sollemnia* to describe the eucharist, it was often qualified by the plural genitive form *missarum* (of the Mass) as, for example, when Pope St Gregory the Great referred to celebrating the solemnities of the Mass (*missarum solemnia celebrarentur*) in 594 AD.[54] Jungmann argues that, in late Latin, the term *missa* is derived from *missio* and *dismissio* in the sense of the formal dismissal and blessing that concluded both the Mass of catechumens and the Mass itself. He also notes that, when it was applied to the eucharist from the middle of the fifth century, *missa* was 'employed mostly in the plural, *missae*, or with some addition, *missarum sollemnia*.'[55] Fortesque suggests that using the plural form, *missarum*, when referring to a single Mass, may have been 'a memory of the old two "masses," of the catechumens and of the faithful.'[56] By the twelfth and thirteenth centuries, the expression *missarum sollemnia* had become one of

---

50. See Boyce O.Carm, *Carmelite Liturgical Spirituality*, p 14

51. Leo F. Stelten, *Dictionary of Ecclesiastical Latin*, trs, ed, Peabody, Massachusetts, Hendrickson, 1995, p 249. It may be that *sollemne* (singular) and *sollemnia* (plural) were originally the singular and plural neuter form of the adjective qualifying the neuter plural nouns *caerimonium* and *caerimonia* (understood), meaning 'solemn (ceremony / ceremonies).'

52. See Tertullian, *de fuga* 14 (PL 2:119)

53. See Cyprian, *de lapsis* 25 (PL 4:485)

54. See Gregory the Great, *Dialogi de vita et miraculis patrum Italicorum* 3:30 (PL 77:288)

55. Jungmann SJ, *Missarum Sollemnia* 1:222-224 = Jungmann SJ, *The Mass of the Roman Rite*, pp 132-133

56. Fortesque, *The Mass. A Study of the Roman Liturgy*, p. 400

the usual ways of referring to the Mass[57] and, generally speaking, it does not seem to have been used in relation to a particular form of the Mass.

Neither the Rule of the Canons Regular of Mortara, of which Albert was a member, nor the surviving section (October to April) of the Liturgical Customs of the Canons Regular of Mortara, use the expression 'solemnities of the Mass (*missarum solemnia*)' found in Albert's *Formula of Life*. On a number of occasions, these documents refer to 'singing/chanting Mass' (*missas cantare*),[58] noting that, at least on occasion, 'the cantors begin the Mass (*cantor[es] incipiant missam*).'[59] It is possible that these references to singing at Mass refer to the *missa cantata*, a simple sung Mass with a congregation celebrated by a presbyter with a second cleric present as a rule, generally a deacon.[60] A simple *missa cantata* seems unlikely, however, given the reference to announcing 'the offices [i.e. roles played by different individuals] for Mass (*nuncientur … misse officia*),'[61] and the instruction 'let them celebrate becomingly a Mass in which no-one should dare to assign singing unless they are wearing white vestments (*honeste celebrent missam in qua nemo audeat imponere cantum nisi in albis vestibus*).'[62] It seems more likely that the chanting/singing was part of the solemn celebration of the conventual Mass of the Canons of Mortara, the *maior missa*, which is mentioned on a

---

57. See See Gratian's *Concordia Discordantium Canorum* 3.1.30; Thomas Aquinas, *Summa theologiae* III q 80, a 8 ad 6. See also Deferrari, Barry CDP, and McGuiness OP, *A Lexicon of St Thomas Aquinas*, p 1036
58. See appendix 1, 'La regola dei Mortariensi' in Mosca O Carm, *Alberto*, pp 561-597 at 582/774; appendix 2, 'Le Consuetudini Mortariensi' in Mosca O Carm, *Alberto*, pp 599-617 at 611/581, 613/688.
59. See appendix 2, 'Le Consuetudini Mortariensi' in Mosca O Carm, *Alberto*, pp 599-617 at 615/771-772
60. Jungmann SJ, *Missarum Sollemnia* 1:263 = Jungmann SJ, *The Mass of the Roman Rite*, pp 153-154
61. See appendix 2, 'Le Consuetudini Mortariensi' in Mosca O Carm, *Alberto*, pp 599-617 at 600/54, 612/626, 617/858-859
62. See appendix 2, 'Le Consuetudini Mortariensi' in ibid, pp 599-617 at 601/72-73

number of different occasions,[63] and which is distinguished from 'the third Mass [of the day] (*tertiam missam*).'[64] The *maior missa* would normally be celebrated in the morning, after Terce and, on at least one occasion, we read that the order 'prescribed by the Missal (*missale ordinata*)' was to be followed.[65] The reference to the 'Mass that is celebrated after None (*missam que celebratur ad nonam*)'[66] is probably also a reference to the conventual *maior missa*, which was celebrated after None on fast days. The reference to acolytes at Mass holding candles 'when ... the sacrifice is offered (*quando ... sacrificium offerendum*)'[67] suggests the context of the solemn celebration of the principal conventual Mass, the *maior missa*.

Apart from that in the *Formula of Life* of the Carmelites, there are three references to *missarum sollemnia* in the documents of which Albert was author or co-author. In 1201, Albert, then Bishop of Vercelli, together with Abbot Peter of Lucedio, were delegated by Pope Innocent to investigate a dispute between the monks and canons of the church of St Ambrose in Milan. The document they produced notes that Abbot Arialdo, on behalf of the monks, had complained to Peter, the *praepositus* (the person in charge) of the canons, that because the canons did not begin their Masses at the right time, the monks were not able to begin their own Masses on time.[68] In their judgement, Bishop Albert and Abbot Peter say that, 'where it concerns the Solemnities of

63. See appendix 2, 'Le Consuetudini Mortariensi' in ibid, pp 599-617 at 600/61, 605/276-277, 611/566-567, 612/620, 616/799, 617/847

64. See *'missam que celebratur ad nonam,'* *'tertiam missam,'* and *'celebrent missam de nativitate'* in appendix 2, 'Le Consuetudini Mortariensi' in ibid, pp 599-617 at 617/856

65. See appendix 2, 'Le Consuetudini Mortariensi' in ibid, pp 599-617 at 612/606.

66. See *'missam que celebratur ad nonam,'* *'tertiam missam,'* and *'celebrent missam de nativitate'* in appendix 2, 'Le Consuetudini Mortariensi' in ibid, pp 599-617 at 617/846-847

67. See appendix 1, 'La regola dei Mortariensi' in ibid, pp 561-597 at 563/75

68. See appendix 4, *sentenza* 5, 'Le Consuetudini Mortariensi' in ibid, pp 635-639 at 636/48-49

the Mass (*ubi de Missarum Solemniis agitur*),' the canons must not prolong their services unduly, and must begin their Masses on time.[69] The monks of St Ambrose were to ring the bells for their major (conventual) Mass (*ad Missam Maiorem*) at their customary time and they should celebrate their conventual Mass at the same time that the other monks of their order were accustomed 'to celebrate the solemnities of the Mass (*Missarum Solemnia celebrare*).'[70] In this document, the expression 'Solemnities of the Mass (*missarum solemnia*)' cannot simply mean 'Mass.' It seems to be used as an alternative way of referring to the celebration of the principal conventual Masses (the *missa maior*) of the canons and of the monks of St Ambrose.

There is another reference to 'the solemnities of the Mass (*missarum solemnia*)' in the Privilege of Approval of the First Order of the Humiliati (16 June 1201), which Albert had helped to draft. The First Order was limited to clerics and, having transformed them into a community of canons regular, they are described as sharing in all the obligations and privileges of such canons. Among the liturgical privileges listed, the Privilege of Approval says that their presbyters, together with their deacons and subdeacons, 'may licitly celebrate the solemnities of the Mass (*licite possint Missarum solemnis celebrare*),' following the usage (*consuetudinem*) of the canons regular of Mortara.[71] The references to presbyters, deacons and subdeacons all being involved in the celebration suggests that a solemn liturgy was envisaged and, given Albert's use of the term 'solemnities of the Mass (*missarum sollemnia*)' that same year (1201) to refer to the principal conventual Masses of the canons and monks of St Ambrose, it seems likely that the First Order of the Humiliati were being allowed to celebrate a similar solemn conventual

---

69. See appendix 4, *sentenza* 5, 'Le Consuetudini Mortariensi' in ibid, pp 635-639 at 637/96-100

70. See appendix 4, *sentenza* 5, 'Le Consuetudini Mortariensi' in ibid, pp 635-639 at 637/102-105

71. See appendix 6, 'Privilegio di Approvazione de Primo Ordine degli Umiliati' in ibid, pp 655-659 at 657/85. See also Mosca O Carm, *Alberto*, p 316

Mass. The surviving 'Usages of the Canons of Mortara (*Consuetudines Mortarienses*)' show that the daily celebration of a conventual major Mass (*maior missa*) was presumed.

All three of the references to the solemnities of the Mass (*missarum solemnia*) in these documents are concerned with the conventual Mass (*missa maior*) of the group in question. There does not seem to be a valid reason for thinking that Albert envisaged something different in the case of the hermits on Mount Carmel and this impression would appear to be confirmed by his prescription that they were to gather in the morning each day to hear it. As a rule, the conventual Mass was a high or solemn Mass (*missa sollemnis*) accompanied by chanting / singing by a choir and, according to Jungmann,[72] the norms for such Masses up to the tenth or eleventh centuries mentioned a number of deacons and subdeacons but, from that point on, only one deacon and one subdeacon accompanies the priest as he proceeds to the altar. Boyce comments that, since there is no mention of bringing in a celebrant from outside the community, 'at least one early Carmelite was ordained.'[73] However, if Albert did indeed have the norms of a solemn conventual Mass in mind, it seems likely that, not only was there at least one ordained priest in the community, but that there was also at least one deacon and one subdeacon. It is, of course, possible (and, indeed, likely) that those who acted as deacon and subdeacon may themselves have been ordained as presbyters.

Mass According to the Rite of the Holy Sepulchre
Noting that 'Virtually all Carmelite liturgical manuscripts refer to the [Carmelite] rite as following that of the Holy Sepulchre,'[74] Boyce suggests that 'One can safely presume that the first Carmelites followed the rite of the Holy Sepulchre as concerns the ordering of the liturgical year and the details of each day's

---

72. Jungmann SJ, *Missarum Sollemnia* 1:256 = Jungmann SJ, *The Mass of the Roman Rite*, p 150
73. See Boyce O Carm, *Carmelite Liturgical Spirituality*, p 14
74. See ibid, p 16

observance.'[75] The rite of the Holy Sepulchre was the local usage
in the Latin Patriarchate of Jerusalem at the time and it took its
name from the church in Jerusalem believed to be the site of the
Lord's burial place. A new Church of the Holy Sepulchre had
been built on the original site by the crusaders in the Romanesque
style typical of Europe at that time, and a community of the
Canons Regular of the Holy Sepulchre had been established
there in 1099. When Jerusalem was captured by the Saracens in
1187, both the Latin Patriarch of Jerusalem and the Canons
Regular of the Holy Sepulchre, moved to Acre near the coast.[76]
In 1205, when Soffredo (Godfrey), the Cardinal of Saint
Praxedes who was Latin Patriarch of Jerusalem from 1202-1205,
resigned his post, the mostly French and Italian Canons Regular
of the Holy Sepulchre, based in Acre, postulated Albert as the
new Patriarch. The local church in Acre served as his cathedral
in place of his Patriarchal Basilica of the Holy Sepulchre in
Jerusalem, and the chapter of the Canons Regular of the Holy
Sepulchre, who had postulated him as Patriarch, also resided in
that same church. As a member of the Canons Regular of
Martara, Albert was probably very much at home with these
Canons Regular of the Holy Sepulchre who, having adopted a
version of the rule of Saint Augustine in 1114,[77] belonged, as he
did, to the large family of the Canons of St Augustine.

The rite of the Holy Sepulchre was an adaptation of French
rites for the celebration of the eucharist in the light of the
Augustinian Rule of the Canons Regular of the Holy Sepulchre.
It was characterised by 'a series of unique feasts relating to Holy
Land personages and events, including for instance the entrance
of Noah into the Ark,' the feast of the Transfiguration on 6
August, the feast of the patriarchs Abraham, Isaac and Jacob on

75. See ibid, p 14
76. See M. Hereswitha, 'Canonici Regolari del S. Sepolcro,' in *Dizionario
degli Istituti de Perfezione*, translated, 14 vols, Rome, 1961-1987, 2:148-151
77. See Boyce O Carm, *Carmelite Liturgical Spirituality*, p 14; Hugo
Buchtal, *Miniature Painting in the Latin Kingdom of Jerusalem*, Oxford,
1957

6 October, and the commemoration of the resurrection,[78] celebrated on the last Sunday of the liturgical year in November.[79]
One of the responsaries for the feast of St Mary Magdalene (the
herald of the resurrection), *Optimam partem*, refers to Mary as
having chosen the better part (contemplation) in comparison to
her sister, Martha.[80] It also highlighted the feasts associated with
both Paul (the Conversion of Paul and the Commemoration of
Saint Paul) and Peter (the Chair of Peter, Saints Peter and Paul).[81]
The fact that some of these unique feasts carried over into the
Carmelite liturgy lends strong support for Boyce's thesis that the
rite of the Holy Sepulchre was used by the first hermit brothers
on Mount Carmel.[82] The emphasis on personages associated
with the Holy Land in the Rite of the Holy Sepulchre may also
have had some bearing on the evolution of liturgical feasts in
honour of the Old Testament prophets, Elijah and Elisha.

The Chapter on the Eucharist in the Rule of Pope Innocent IV (1247)
When Albert's *Formula of Life* was revised and adapted before
being formally approved as a rule for religious by Pope Innocent
IV in 1247, only minor orthographic and grammatical changes
were made to chapter 14 of Albert's text:

Innocent's Rule (Latin):
Oratorium, prout commodius fieri
poterit, construatur in medio cellu-
larum, ubi 'mane per singulos
dies' (Lev 6:12, Vulgate) ad audienda missarum sollemnia convenire debeatis, ubi commode fieri
potest.

Innocent's Rule (Translation):
According as it will have been
possible to be done more conveniently, an oratory is to be built in
the middle of the cells where,
when it is possible to be done conveniently, you ought to gather 'in
the morning each day' (Lev 6:12,
Vulgate) for hearing the solemnities of the Mass.

---

78. See Benedict Mary of the Cross Zimmerman OCD, *Ordinaire de
l'Ordre de Notre-Dame du Mont Carmel par Sibert de Beka (vers 1312) publié
d'après le manuscrit original et collationné sur divers manuscrits et imprimés*,
Paris, 1910, pp 37-39
79. See Boyce O Carm, *Carmelite Liturgical Spirituality*, pp 14, 19-20
80. See ibid, p 22
81. See ibid, p 23
82. See ibid, p 14; Buchtal, *Miniature Painting*; Zimmerman OCD, *Ordinaire*

The various other changes introduced by Pope Innocent's Rule, and the changed context brought about by the move to Europe that had taken place during the previous decade, meant that the chapter on the eucharist had taken on a somewhat different significance. The introduction of the recitation of the canonical hours in common (see chapter 11) meant, presumably, that as well as being the place for Mass and the weekly meeting for the correction of faults, the oratory in each of their foundations, on Mount Carmel and elsewhere, was now also the place for the daily celebration of the different canonical hours. Pope Innocent IV's letter to diocesan bishops, *Frequens paganorum incursus*, dated 1 October 1247, directed them to permit the Carmelites to use a bell 'so that, scattered in their cells, they may come together for divine worship'. Presumably, the bell was used to call the hermit brothers from their sometimes widely separated cells for the recitation of the canonical hours, and presumbaly also for Mass, at specified times each day. Most of the groups who recited the canonical hours in common also had a daily celebration of the eucharist and the hermit brothers of Mount Carmel now conformed to this norm.[83] A daily community Mass, with the presumption of receiving communion, was normative for the male[84] branches of the Mendicant movement then emerging in Europe.[85] St Francis exhorted his friars to have only one Mass each day and, because concelebration was not then possible, the other priests in the community were encouraged to participate in the celebration of the priest in question.[86] By 1274, the expression *Missa conventualis* (celebrated in a public

---

83. See Vrakking O Carm, 'Albert's Formula for Living' at 31 n 49
84. Daily Mass was not the norm in the female and lay branches of that movement. The Poor Clares, by their rule of 1219, communicated six times a year while the Second and Third Order of St Dominic communicated only fifteen and four times a year, respectively.
85. See P. Sawicki, *De missa conventuali*, Crakow, 1938, 2 nn 12, 16, 17
86. See St Francis of Assisi, 'Lettera al capitolo generale e a tutti i frati' in *Fonte Franciscani. Scritti e biografie di san Francesco d'Assisi. Cronache e altre testimonianze del primo secolo francescano. Scritti e biografie di santa Chiara d'Assisi*, Assisi, Padova, Edizioni Messaggero Padova, 1977, 1980, p 162

gathering, or *conventus*, of the members of the community) had generally replaced the monastic term 'major Mass (*maior missa*).'[87] Vrakking/Smet comment that, among the Carmelites, 'Until the sixteenth century, one brother, usually the prior or provincial, presided at the eucharist while the others attended Mass, unless one had to say Mass outside the convent.'[88]

The Rite of the Holy Sepulchre was not known in Europe when the Carmelites began to settle there about 1235, and Boyce comments that the local usage presumed on Mount Carmel 'now had to be defined and explained, since this rite was not generally known outside the Latin Kingdom' of Jerusalem.[89] He suggests that this liturgical difference 'must have given the European Carmelites a sense of being set apart from other Orders, since their liturgy blended both eastern and western influences. Boyce suggests that, borrowing much material from the Dominican tradition,[90] a distinct Carmelite Rite gradually evolved from the Holy Sepulchre Rite.

In 1312 the Ordinal compiled by Sibert de Beka[91] was published by the General Chapter of London and, according to Boyce, the texts it specified 'for Mass each day ... established absolute liturgical uniformity throughout the entire Order.'[92] According to Jungmann,[93] the ceremonial for the celebration of Mass in the Ordinal of Sibert de Beka was 'a slight modification' of the Dominican 'Ordinary according to the Rite of the Sacred Order of Friars Preachers' that had been produced under the Dominican General, Humbert de Romans, and enacted into law in 1256. One of the interesting features of Sibert de Beka's Ordinal, derived from the Holy Sepulchre liturgy, was that the

87. See Sawicki, *De missa conventuali* 2 n 6

88. See Vrakking O Carm, 'Albert's Formula for Living' at 31 n 49

89. See Boyce O Carm, *Carmelite Liturgical Spirituality*, p 16

90. See W. R. Bonniwell, *A History of the Dominican Liturgy, 1215-1945*, New York, 1945

91. See the critical edition in Zimmerman OCD, *Ordinaire*.

92. Boyce O Carm, *Carmelite Liturgical Spirituality*, p 17

93. Jungmann SJ, *Missarum Sollemnia* 1:128 = Jungmann SJ, *The Mass of the Roman Rite*, p 75

celebrant did not kneel at the consecration, which was the uni-
versal custom elsewhere, but only bowed his head. While the
bowed head reflected the death of Christ on the cross, the standing posture, presumably, reflected the typical stance of the risen
Christ on whom the Holy Sepulchre liturgy was centred.

The Eucharistic Spirituality of the Carmelite Rule

As we look back to our origins after more than 750 years, what
should we recognise as the authentic eucharistic spirituality of
our Carmelite Rule? There are, I think, four important elements.
Firstly, there is the spirituality of gathering as a community to
hear the Liturgy of the Word together and to participate collect-
ively in the Liturgy of the Eucharist so that we may 'put on the
armour of God' and 'be able to hold out against the ambushes of
the enemy' (see chapter 18). Secondly, by quoting the text of Lev
6:12, where the Old Testament priests replenish the sacrificial
fire with wood 'in the morning each day' to ensure that it never
goes out, Albert seems to have made a deliberate association between the eucharist and the burnt sacrifices of the Old
Testament and, in particular, between the way in which our
daily eucharist enables us to make a perpetual sacrifice of prayer
and the way in which replenishing the wood of the perpetual
fire each morning ensured that the offering of sacrifice was continual. We are called to nourish and renew the continual spiritual
offering of our minds and hearts in the service of our risen Lord,
Jesus Christ (see chapter 2), each morning at Mass. Thirdly, by
prescribing a solemn conventual Mass (*missarum sollemnia*),
Albert invites us to celebrate our daily Mass with proper solem-
nity and with appropriate chanting or singing because it is the
primary moment of our daily encounter with Jesus, the one
Saviour, who saves 'his people from their sins' (see chapter 19).
Fourthly, because the hermit-brothers both adopted the rite of
the Holy Sepulchre as celebrated in their Patriarch's own church
at Acre and later adapted that rite in accordance with European
norms, we should try to find the proper balance between our
own Carmelite liturgical traditions and the norms and rites approved by the local hierarchy.

List of Contributors

ELTIN GRIFFIN O CARM is a liturgist, retreat director and preacher.

BRIAN MCKAY O CARM holds an M Phil from the Irish School of Ecumenics. He is Sub-Prior at Gort Muire, Dublin, and is a well-known organist and preacher.

SISTER TERESA WHELAN ODC is a member of the Discalced Carmelite Community at Roebuck, Dublin 4. She is a nature lover and beekeeper.

JOE MOTHERSILL O CARM is a graduate of the Washington Theological Union. He is engaged in formation and pastoral work at Gort Muire, Dublin.

CHRIS O'DONNELL O CARM is attached to the Milltown Institute where he lectures in various aspects of spirituality including mysticism. Author of *Ecclesia*, an encyclopedia of the church and of a number of books on mariology, prayer and the church.

PHILIP MCPARLAND ODC lives at the Carmelite Spirituality Institute at Avila, Donnybrook, Dublin, where he is engaged in formation and retreat work.

MÍCEÁL O'NEILL O CARM is Prior of Terenure College, Dublin. He has had vast experience of ministry in Peru. His doctoral thesis in Rome was on the emerging spirituality in Peru.

PAT MULLINS O CARM is Dean of Theology at the Milltown Institute. He is a theologian and expert on medieval Carmelite history.